AF291083

THE FORGOTTEN HEROES OF THE
BRITISH SUFFRAGE MOVEMENT

THE FORGOTTEN HEROES OF THE BRITISH SUFFRAGE MOVEMENT

The People, Themes and Events that Shaped the Fight for Women's Right to Vote in the United Kingdom

ANDREW GRIFFITHS

PEN & SWORD HISTORY

AN IMPRINT OF PEN & SWORD BOOKS LTD.
YORKSHIRE – PHILADELPHIA

First published in Great Britain in 2026 by
PEN AND SWORD HISTORY
An imprint of
Pen & Sword Books Ltd
Yorkshire – Philadelphia

ISBN 978 1 03611 649 1

Typeset in Times New Roman 12/16 by
SJmagic DESIGN SERVICES, India.
Printed and bound in the UK by CPI Group (UK) Ltd.

The Publisher's authorised representative in the EU for product safety is
Authorised Rep Compliance Ltd., Ground Floor, 71 Lower Baggot Street,
Dublin D02 P593, Ireland.
www.arccompliance.com

For a complete list of Pen & Sword titles please contact
PEN & SWORD BOOKS LIMITED
George House, Units 12 & 13, Beevor Street, Off Pontefract Road,
Barnsley, South Yorkshire, S71 1HN, England
E-mail: enquiries@pen-and-sword.co.uk
Website: www.pen-and-sword.co.uk

or

PEN AND SWORD BOOKS
1950 Lawrence Rd, Havertown, PA 19083, USA
E-mail: uspen-and-sword@casematepublishers.com
Website: www.penandswordbooks.com

Author Biography

Andrew Griffiths is an independent researcher who has been studying the past for over twenty years. He graduated with a History Degree in 2007 and began a career as a freelance writer the following year. In 2012, he launched *historyoffighting.com*, a website dedicated to teaching the history of martial arts, combat sports and military history. He has also authored a book called *The Birth of the Samurai*, which charts the development of the warrior elite in early Japanese society.

Disclaimer

It is believed that all quotes, photographs and illustrations used in this book are within the public domain or fall under fair usage rights. If you believe your copyrighted work has been used without your permission and fair usage does not apply, please contact the publisher so that the work may be fully credited and acknowledged in any future reprint of this book.

Contents

Introduction

When we think of the concept of female suffrage in the United Kingdom, we often associate it with the struggles of the early twentieth century. However, by this time, the idea was far from new as it was being discussed and written about as far back as the mid-eighteenth century, although at that time it was primarily regarded as nothing more than a quaint idea. The patriarch of the household was typically responsible for making important decisions on behalf of the entire family and this included voting, although many men were also unfranchised as participating in elections was a privilege reserved for the wealthy.

The seeds of change were sown in the nineteenth century when the first petition for women's suffrage was presented to Parliament in 1832. By the middle of the century, the first suffrage societies began to emerge, and campaigners would meet with politicians, produce literature to put forward their ideas, and lobby the government to propose parliamentary bills that would allow women to become a part of the electorate. While these measures seem mild to us today, the fact that the perpetrators were women would have left many in Victorian society, both men and women, stunned because at the time it would have been considered radical activism.

Although there was a level of unity, disagreements were a regular occurrence causing many splits within the suffrage societies from very early on and throughout the period. Probably the most significant of these separations occurred when the Women's Social and Political Union

(WSPU) split from the National Union of Women's Suffrage Societies (NUWSS) in 1903, marking the rise of militant suffrage campaigners. The acts of vandalism and violence, and the arrests and prison terms of the militants stand out as the most interesting aspects of the suffrage movement. Nevertheless, it should be remembered that this was arrived at from a gradual escalation and only after more peaceful methods of protest had consistently failed. The militant campaigners would risk their reputations, their freedom and even face injury and death when they called out MPs, faced hostile crowds and damaged property as a part of their fight for the right to vote on the same terms as men.

The lives of some of the leading members of the WSPU and NUWSS have been well-documented over the years. However, *The Forgotten Heroes of the British Suffrage Movement* aims to highlight a small number of the less famous women who worked tirelessly to bring about a fairer society, while also investigate the themes, issues and events that affected them and their activism. Some were themselves leaders who organised, made speeches and led marches, while others were from the rank and file and focused on the less glamorous aspects of the movement, such as selling newspapers, handing out written literature, and attending the numerous marches and protests held by the various suffrage groups.

Propaganda played a significant role in spreading the message, and various types of media were utilised, including posters, flyers, articles, artworks and attention-grabbing stunts that would often make headlines in the national, and sometimes even international, newspapers. As the press was often hostile to the suffrage societies, many wrote and published their own newspapers to ensure their message was heard in their own words, while also helping to raise much-needed funds. As more people became aware of, and concerned about, the issues, an increasing number of people joined the fight.

Although it was predominantly a movement of the middle classes, it was soon realised that the support of the multitudes of working-class women was needed so propaganda was often aimed at them. It was also understood that this type of campaigning could prove expensive so women from the upper class also proved invaluable to the cause; not only did they provide funding, they often had the ear of influential men such as Lords and Members of Parliament. Many people were against the concept of allowing women to vote and so anti-suffrage groups also formed. The propaganda campaigns of the anti-suffrage groups followed the same lines as that of their opponents; they demonstrated, marched, and produced art and literature in an attempt to undermine the suffrage movement.

Starting in 1905, the militant tactics of the WSPU led to arrests, and numerous members would be imprisoned over the years. Furious that they were not being treated as political prisoners, many suffragettes protested by going on hunger strike. The government and prison services countered this with force-feeding, a barbaric practice that was previously used only in insane asylums; this turned some of the public onto the side of the suffrage campaigners, or at least against the anti-suffrage authorities. The militancy reached new heights from 1911, and arson attacks and bombings became a regular occurrence in the so-called 'reign of terror' orchestrated by the WSPU. This only ceased with the onset of the First World War in 1914, when most militant actions and suffrage protests came to a halt, and many of the women involved turned their attention to supporting the war effort.

Today, we tend to see the movement in binary terms with the militant and sometimes violent WSPU on one side, and the more law-abiding suffragists of the NUWSS on the other. But the story of the fight for women's enfranchisement is much more complicated. There were many organisations and splinter groups, and individuals would often belong to more than one of these simultaneously. Moreover, militant and constitutional suffrage organisations frequently worked, marched and protested together. Individually, women who would usually be divided by socioeconomic background, race, partisan affiliation and ethical and moral beliefs, would work together, and while there was some conflict between them, campaigners for the most part respected and supported one another in the fight to obtain the vote for women.

CHAPTER ONE

The Early Suffrage Movement

Although many people associate the suffrage movement with Emmeline Pankhurst and her militant suffragettes in the early twentieth century, it actually began decades earlier as a much more peaceful movement. As far back as the late eighteenth century, Mary Wollstonecraft (mother of *Frankenstein* author Mary Shelley), was calling for the right for women to vote in her 1792 work, *A Vindication of the Rights of Woman*, though in it she was quick to point out, 'I do not wish [women] to have power over men; but over themselves.' At this time, most working-class men could not vote, so the concept of women being involved in politics and law-making was laughable to many. This remained the case going into the nineteenth century, as it was widely believed that husbands, fathers or other male guardians were responsible for making such decisions on behalf of women.

By the 1820s the issue of who should be entitled to enfranchisement had become a contentious topic. Only 3 per cent of men had voting rights at this time, and with the memory of the French Revolution (1789–1799) still fresh in their minds, the government realised that something needed to be done. The Great Reform Act of 1832 (also known as the Representation of the People Act, the Reform Act 1832, or the First Reform Act) led to the enfranchisement of many men in Britain, with the number of eligible men rising by an estimated 7 per cent.

The actual number of people who could vote is difficult to establish, as there was no voter registration in place. However, it is estimated that before 1832, around 400,000 to 500,000 people could vote, and after that the number rose to around 600,000 to 800,000. Despite the progress being made, no women were included in the new voting rights, and the term 'male' was for the first time added to the definition of a voter.

MP Henry Hunt had introduced a petition to include the enfranchisement of a small number of women in the bill, specifically unmarried women from the higher social classes who owned property. Although his efforts failed, the idea of female suffrage had now been presented to Parliament, and it would remain a mainstay of political debate until universal suffrage was finally achieved in Britain in 1928.

Barbara Bodichon – The Original Feminist Organiser

Barbara Leigh Smith Bodichon (1827–1891) was born in East Sussex, where she spent much of her time in Hastings. Her father, Benjamin Leigh Smith, was the only son of William Smith, the famous MP and abolitionist who also had four daughters, (one of whom, Frances 'Fanny' Smith, would become the mother of Florence Nightingale). Her mother was a hat maker called Anne Longden, and although her parents had five children they never married, choosing instead to live openly together 'in sin'. The reason for this is unclear, and while it's true that a member of the land-owning gentry marrying a girl from a lower social order would have caused a scandal, it would have been a much bigger taboo for them to live together as a family without being married. It has been speculated that the reason for this was because Benjamin did not want Anne to become the equivalent of his property, which would have been the case under marriage law at the time. As a radical liberal, this would undoubtedly align with his beliefs and he further broke with tradition by treating his male and female children equally in terms of finances; when each of them reached 21 years old, they received a £300 annual allowance.

Most women of Bodichon's social status were expected to marry and have children, but she was raised to believe she could live her life as she saw fit. She studied art, political economy, and law at Bedford Square, and in addition to her interest in social reform, she also became a painter and a writer. Her watercolours, many of which were exhibited at the Salon and the Royal Academy of Arts, were, and still are, highly regarded in the art world, and from 1848 she wrote articles on women's issues under her pen name 'Esculapius', which were published in the *Hastings and St Leonards News*. From 1850 she spent her time between Hastings and London, focusing on her art and socialising with artists and her bohemian friends when in Hastings. While in the capital, however, she concentrated more on activism and her progressive friends.

In the mid-nineteenth century, if a wife earned or inherited property it belonged to her husband, who could use it as he saw fit. Her primary goal was to change this by advocating for reform regarding a woman's right to own property, which was considered a radical idea at the time as many believed it would create problems between married couples and disrupt the 'natural' order of society. Bodichon managed to gather around 26,000 signatures to present to the House of Lords in March 1856 and petition for a change in the law. Although it was inevitably rejected, it was arguably the first large-scale, organised action taken by feminists in the UK.

In 1857, Barbara met and married Eugène Bodichon, who was as radical and forward-thinking as she was. A year later, she, along with her close friend Bessie Rayner Parks, founded the *English Women's Journal*, which published articles calling for women's rights, including the right to vote. She helped found the Kensington Society in 1865, which included Emily Davis, Lydia Becker and Elizabeth Garrett, sister of Millicent Garrett Fawcett. In 1866, the group persuaded the MPs John Stuart Mill, Henry Fawcett (the future husband of Millicent Garrett Fawcett) and Peter Alfred Taylor to include an amendment in their 1867 Reform Act that would grant equal political rights for women as well as men.

When the idea of female suffrage was first introduced as part of the bill, Edward Kent Karslake, the Conservative MP for Colchester, spoke out against the amendment, stating that he had not heard of any women in Essex who wanted the right to vote. This prompted the committee members to gather a petition signed by around 1,500 women, all of whom agreed that they would like to be included in the electorate. This petition was the first of its kind, but by no means the last. Perhaps unsurprisingly, when Mill presented it to Parliament to support the act, it was not enough, and the amendment was defeated with seventy-three votes in favour and 196 against. Bodichon wrote a now-famous article in which she stated:

> That a respectable, orderly, independent body in the state should have no voice, and no influence recognised by the law, in the election of the representatives of the people, while they are otherwise acknowledged as responsible citizens, are eligible for many public offices, and required to pay all taxes, is an anomaly which seems to require some explanation.
>
> Barbara Bodichon. *Reasons for the Enfranchisement of Women*. National Association for the Promotion of Social Science (1866).

Two years later in 1867, the Kensington Society was rebranded as the London National Society for Women's Suffrage (LNSWS), which formed a loose federation with similar groups based in Manchester and Edinburgh. These were collectively called the National Society for Women's Suffrage (NSWS), which is regarded as the precursor to the main suffrage groups that emerged over the ensuing decades.

Barbara Bodichon was a forerunner in the fight for women's enfranchisement and several other aspects of the women's movement. She helped bring about change for women's property rights, founded educational institutions for women – especially those from lower socioeconomic backgrounds – and fought for women's right to work and keep their own earnings. She was a major influence on, and virtually founded, the women's rights movement in Britain but is largely forgotten today. She died on 11 June 1891 and was buried in St Thomas à Becket Church in Brightling, East Sussex. Despite all she achieved, she is not even mentioned in the church's guidebook of notable people buried there, although her brother, Arctic explorer Benjamin Leigh Smith, is.

Lydia Becker – The Unofficial Leader of the Suffrage Movement

Lydia Ernestine Becker (1827–1890) came from a well-off family and was the daughter of a chemical works owner in the city of Manchester. Her mother died in 1855, so most of the responsibility of raising her fourteen younger siblings fell on her. As a young woman, Becker's passion was science; she was an award-winning botanist and in 1867, she started a group called the Manchester Ladies' Literacy Society, which, despite its name, was intended to allow women to study scientific matters at a time when this would have been frowned upon by many of her contemporaries. After hearing a lecture given by Barbara Bodichon in 1866, Becker was convinced of the idea of women's suffrage, and this soon became her new life mission. As a member of the Kensington Society, she helped get the amendment to the 1867 Reform Act that would allow some women to vote. She later wrote of the failure to get it passed:

> What might have been gained during this time had women succeeded in establishing their claim to the suffrage … can never now be known, but we believe that had this been effected there would have been more just laws regarding the property and maintenance of wife, more complete recognition of the sacred rights of mothers, more efficient protection for the maimed and miserable victims of the murderous outrages on wives, more freedom to engage in professional and industrial occupations for the increasing number of women who must depend on their work for their living, more scope

for the energies of women who do not need to work for their livelihood in public affairs, such as the relief of the poor, the supervision of workhouses, parochial schools, and prisons where women are immured.

In short, there would have been more progress in every direction in which women have been seeking to improve their own condition and to render service to the community. For women do not ask for their rights in order to further selfish interests or with a view to forsaking their natural duties. They ask for their rights in the interests of the community, and in order that they may better perform the duties that devolve upon them as members of the family and citizens of the State.

Lydia Becker. *Words of a Leader*.
The Central Society for
Women's Suffrage (1904).

Lilly Maxwell was a shopkeeper and a ratepayer but, as a woman, she was shocked to find that her name had been added to the voting register in Manchester by mistake. She requested Becker's assistance and on polling day in 1867 they went to the Town Hall where Maxwell was permitted to vote. The January 1868 edition of the *Englishwoman's Review* reported in an article called 'The Case of Lily Maxwell':

It is sometimes said that women, especially those of the working class, have no political opinion at all, and would not care to vote. Yet this woman, who by chance was furnished with a vote, professed strong political opinions, and was delighted to have a chance of expressing them … Mrs Maxwell's name being on the list of electors, the returning officer had no choice in the matter, but was bound to accept her vote. As soon as it was given, the other voters in the room … united in three hearty cheers for the heroine of the day.

After this, the suffragists attempted to encourage other tax-paying women to register, and Becker led over 7,700 women to claiming their right to vote. However, in 1868 it was declared illegal to allow any women to participate in the democratic process, so what seemed like an early victory for the women's movement turned into a loss. Despite the setback, there would be positive advancements for women over the next few years. In 1870, the Married Women's Property Act was passed. It was drafted by Richard Pankhurst, the future husband of Emmeline, and meant that women could earn money and own property independently, with their husbands having no claim to it. The Education Act of 1870 opened the doors for women to vote for, and serve on, school boards, a change of which Becker took full advantage. She had been very critical of how girls were educated in Manchester and thought that boys should learn domestic tasks, such as cooking their own food and mending their own socks.

In 1870, MP William Forsyth proposed a bill that would grant the right to vote to single women but exclude married women. Although it caused some controversy within the movement, the unmarried Becker was supportive of it as she saw it as a temporary measure and believed it would serve as a step in the right direction. She argued that the fight would continue until women had the same voting rights as men, but many members of the movement were enraged by this and she was forced to resign from the Married Women's Property Committee later that year. Becker would ultimately be forgiven and despite this perceived indiscretion, her peers often regarded her as the unofficial leader of the suffrage movement in the late nineteenth century.

Becker was friends with leading radicals of the time including Richard Pankhurst, a fellow member of the committee known as the Manchester Society for Women's Suffrage (MSWS), for which she was the secretary. Another of her friends was Jacob Bright, co-founder of the MSWS (along with Elizabeth Wolstenholme), who was a Liberal MP and an ally of the movement. He secured an amendment that granted women the right to vote in municipal elections and later, Bright and Becker saw success in the Isle of Man when they campaigned to have women included in the 1881 House of Keys elections. Becker stated of the success in winning some votes in local elections:

> Now that women are admitted as eligible for these public positions – now that they are placed on the burgess rolls in municipal districts and sent to the ballot box every year to take part in popular elections, what can be said against the proposal to extend to these enrolled citizens the right to vote once in four or five years in the election of a Parliamentary representative? … It cannot refuse our claim on the plea that women ought not to vote in popular elections, for it has recently admitted them to such vote. It cannot refuse on the plea that women are legally incapacitated for every political function, for the highest political function known to the Constitution is discharged by a woman. The present political status of the sex is thoroughly anomalous.
>
> Lydia Becker. *Words of a Leader*.
> The Central Society for
> Women's Suffrage (1904).

The way Becker could influence politicians through her lobbying on behalf of women was unique for the time and would inspire activists for generations to come, including future leaders within the suffrage movement, Millicent Garrett Fawcett and Emmeline Pankhurst. It was only after Becker's death in 1890 that Fawcett became the intellectual leader of the suffrage movement and, arguably, it was the foundations laid by Lydia Becker upon which the two great suffrage campaigners would build to eventually win the vote for British women.

The National Society for Women's Suffrage

As noted, the National Society for Women's Suffrage (NSWS) was formed by Lydia Becker in November 1867 to bring unity and coordination to the country's suffrage organisations. She was the group's first secretary and helped give direction to its parliamentary campaign. The first three groups to join the NSWS were:

- The London National Society for Women's Suffrage (LNSWS) – The LNSWS started life as the Kensington Society and was primarily focused on assisting John Stuart Mill in his campaign to include a women's suffrage amendment in the 1867 Reform Bill.
- The Edinburgh National Society for Women's Suffrage (ENSWS) – The ENSWS was the first group in Scotland to campaign for women's suffrage, believing that anyone paying taxes should have the right to vote. Founding members of the group included Priscilla Bright McLaren, Agnes McLaren, Eliza Wigham, Flora Stevenson and Louisa Stevenson.
- The Manchester National Society for Women's Suffrage (MNSWS) – The MNSWS evolved from the MSWS when it united with the societies from London and Edinburgh. It would undergo other name changes, later becoming the North of England Society for Women's Suffrage and then reverting to its original name, the Manchester Society for Women's Suffrage. Lydia Becker co-founded the MNSWS journal, the *Women's Suffrage Journal* in 1870 along with her fellow activist Jessie Boucherett. Becker was the editor of the publication and so influential was her contribution to it that, upon her death in 1890, it was discontinued.

Each group had its own committee, managed its own finances, and could act independently while benefiting from the support and cooperation of other groups and their members. Many of the campaigners from these organisations had previously been part of the anti-slavery movement and often employed similar tactics and ideas in their suffrage activism. This included, drawing up petitions, holding regular meetings, producing pamphlets, writing essays and journals, and hosting fundraising events.

By the end of the 1860s, London, Manchester and Edinburgh were still the leading centres for suffragists, but meetings were held all over the country. At this time, the various groups shared the same vision and often informed one another about the activities they were to undertake. Other societies that organised over the following years under the umbrella of the NSWS included:

- Bristol and West of England National Women's Suffrage Society (BWNSWS) – Formed in 1868
- Birmingham National Society for Women's Suffrage (BNSWS) – Formed in 1868
- Central Committee of the National Society for Women's Suffrage (CCNSWS) – Formed in *c.*1872
- Central National Society for Women's Suffrage (CNSWS) – Formed in 1888.

In 1871, a split emerged in the suffrage movement, marking the first of many to come. The MNSWS sought to unite all groups with a headquarters located in Manchester, but this was rejected by the London suffragists, who believed the main office should be in the capital. They also objected to the choice of the leader in the north, Jacob Bright, who as MP for Manchester was believed to be in a good position to influence the movement in a way that no woman had the power to do. Individual members also disagreed over which political party they should align themselves with. Some felt the Radical Liberals would take their cause seriously, others favoured the Conservatives and others still had no faith in either party being willing to further their agenda.

There were also disagreements on what specifically should be fought for. Many believed that only single women should get the vote, some wanted the same rights as men and others wanted universal suffrage, meaning all men and women in the county should be allowed to vote (excluding people in prisons and mental health facilities). This division often led women to leave one group and establish a rival group that aligned with their political leanings or beliefs about suffrage. Some of the more prominent breakaway groups included:

- The Women's Franchise League
- The Women's Emancipation Union
- The Cooperative Women's Guild
- The Women's Liberal Federation
- The Primrose League.

A new Reform Bill, known as the Third Reform Bill or the Representation of the People Act, was announced by the Liberal Government in 1884, and many believed that it would afford some women the vote. Although it was not expected to completely satisfy the aims of the suffrage movement, there was an air of optimism that it would at least be a start. When the bill was voted on, it was defeated by a margin of 271 votes to 135. Liberal Prime Minister William Gladstone had spoken against the bill, despite seemingly being in favour of women's suffrage, as he believed the upper-class women who would have gained the vote would likely vote Conservative. The bill was revised and passed at the end of the year, but while it allowed many more men to vote, it did not include any women at all. Before 1832, only 3 per cent of men could vote but by 1885, the number had risen to around 60 per cent.

While there was considerable division within the suffrage movement in the late nineteenth century, this was mainly due to differences in leadership. Most of the women who donated their money, time and energy to the cause were united in their goal to win the vote for women. Many of the campaigners from this time would not live long enough to see victory, but their contribution as pioneers of the suffrage movement cannot be overstated. The movement became more coherent in 1897 with the formation of the NUWSS, to which most major suffrage societies would later merge. In 1872, a 14-year-old girl named Emmeline Goulden attended a meeting of the MNSWS to listen to speakers, and seven years later, she would marry Richard Pankhurst, despite him being twenty-three years her senior. As Emmeline Pankhurst, she would become a member of the NUWSS before leaving in 1903 to found the WSPU, a group that would revolutionise the movement in the twentieth century.

Three Generations of Suffragists – Agnes Pochin, Laura McLaren and Lady Norman

Agnes Pochin (1825–1908) was born Agnes Heap in Timperley, near Manchester, and married Henry Pochin in 1852. She was an early advocate for women's rights and produced a pamphlet titled *The Right of Women to Exercise the Elective Franchise* (1855), outlining what she believed women deserved in terms of rights. Not only did she argue for the right to vote, but she also demanded equal treatment in other areas, such as education and divorce laws. The material was signed with the pen name 'Justitia', and was not reproduced with her real name until 1873. In it, she suggests that women should have, 'The right to vote in the election of Members of Parliament, on the same conditions as the other sex.' She went on to argue that as women have little experience in such matters, they should be allowed to observe the inner workings of 'Both Houses of Parliament to see how public business is actually carried on.'

In 1858, she attempted to persuade the radical and Liberal MP John Bright to include a suffrage clause in his Reform Bill. While he was not personally opposed to it, he rejected the idea because he believed such a clause might reduce the likelihood of his bill being accepted by Parliament. Along with Lydia Becker and Anne Robinson, Pochin was one of the main speakers at a MNSWS meeting at the Free Trade Hall in Manchester on 14 April 1868. The meeting was chaired by her husband Henry, who was the Mayor of Salford at the time, and it is often cited as one of the key events that started the women's suffrage movement in Britain. She joined the CCNSWS in 1872 and contributed not only as a speaker but also as a benefactor, donating substantial sums of money to the CCNSWS and the MNSWS over the years. She retired in 1874 along with her husband and moved to North Wales, where they became active members of the community. Even in retirement, Agnes Pochin continued to be a trailblazer, serving as a Justice of the Peace, Deputy Lieutenant, and Sheriff of Denbighshire while supporting the suffrage activities of her daughter, Laura McLaren.

Born Laura Elizabeth Pochin (1854–1933), she watched the first meeting of the NSWS as a teenager and was hooked. She would go on to be an essential part of the movement herself, becoming an executive member of the NSWS in 1877 and spending much of her time travelling across Britain to talk at meetings and attend rallies. She married Charles Benjamin Bright McLaren in 1877, a Scottish barrister and an MP for Stafford and Bosworth. He came from a long tradition of suffrage campaigners including his parents, his uncle, John Bright, and his grandfather, Jacob Bright. As a campaigner, Laura fought for the rights of all women to vote and be involved in politics. She stated in an article she wrote for the periodical *The Academy* in September 1908:

> Now Sir, I desire to occupy no man's seat. I can, if need be, carry my own garments. I am able to turn door handles and I care not one jot who goes out first. But I do desire for women equal education, equal marriage laws, equal labour laws, and equal political rights. What women hate is not mankind, but man's thoughtless injustice, his complacent satisfaction when he offers women dross for gold and calls it chivalry.

Two years later in 1910, she wrote *The Women's Charter of Rights and Liberties – Preliminary Draft*, which was to be presented to governments worldwide on behalf of the International Woman Suffrage Alliance. In the introduction she said that as Parliament was so congested with increasing matters to attend to, it would be prudent to present, 'In one Act or Charter all the more pressing legal and social grievances of women.' In the same year, McLaren led a group of women to Downing Street to ask the Prime Minister Herbert H. Asquith why he opposed women's rights.

Despite her activism, her husband was made a peer in 1911, giving the couple the titles of Lord and Lady Aberconway. Even though she was a woman of high status, she was never afraid to take on subjects that were not normally discussed in polite conversation. One of her causes was the sexual abuse of young girls and women. She fought for the Criminal Law Amendment Bill (1912), also known as the 'White Slave Traffic Bill', which aimed to stop girls being sold into prostitution. She also believed that all women without the vote were slaves of a kind as they had no say over their destinies, be it politically, in the home or in the workplace.

She founded the Liberal Women's Suffrage Union in 1913, and during the First World War she opened up her house as a nursing home for officers who had sustained injuries, for which she was awarded a CBE (Commander, Order of the British Empire) in 1918 and made Dame of Grace, Order of St John of Jerusalem. When some women were granted the vote in 1918, she continued to advocate for women's rights as a member of the Open-Door Council, an organisation dedicated to securing rights for women in the workplace. She died in 1933 at her home in France, aged 78. Charles and Laura McLaren had four children, two boys who grew up to become Liberal MPs and two daughters, one of whom, Priscilla, married Sir Henry Norman and became a noted activist for the suffrage cause herself.

Florence Priscilla McLaren (1883–1964) was a member of the NUWSS, the Women's Liberal Federation, and would later become the treasurer of the Liberal Women's Suffrage Union. She married the divorcee Sir Norman in 1907 after which she became known as Lady Florence Priscilla Norman, or more commonly Lady Norman. She regularly attended, spoke at and organised meetings for the NUWSS, as well as writing articles and taking part in peaceful protests.

Her husband was a journalist who became a Liberal Member of Parliament in 1900. He supported the suffragist cause and was well respected within it and within politics generally. At one time, he was tipped to become the Foreign Secretary and although he never achieved this, he was knighted in 1906 and served as Postmaster-General for a short time in 1910.

With the outbreak of war in 1914, Lady Norman and her husband ran a hospital in Northern France and on 28 May 1915, she pleaded in the NUWSS newspaper *The Common Cause* for more women, specifically cooks, to come and work in the military hospitals at the front; she was awarded the Mons Star and a CBE for her work during the Great War. She was involved in establishing the Imperial War Museum in 1917 and chaired the Women's Work Sub-Committee, which recorded the work done by women during the conflict. By 1919, the community had collected over 2,500 photographs of women in the workplace and more than 900 photographs of women who had lost their lives or been decorated for their contributions to the Allies' victory. Many of the early items in the collection show a bias towards work carried out by bodies supported by the NUWSS. Despite this, the collection is a vital record of the past and Lady Norman would continue to contribute to it by serving as a trustee for the museum for over forty years.

She represented the rights of women and fought for justice for those who could not fight for themselves for years to come. Among her achievements were serving on the Women's Advisory Committee of the League of Nations and becoming a Justice of the Peace for the children's court in London. She drove a mobile canteen for the Women's Voluntary Service during the air raids on London during the Second World War and was active for most of her life. In 1963, she retired and moved to France, where she died at her home a year later.

> My own sex, I hope, will excuse me, if I treat them like
> rational creatures, instead of flattering their fascinating

graces, and viewing them as if they were in a state of perpetual childhood, unable to stand alone. I earnestly wish to point out in what true dignity and human happiness consists – I wish to persuade women to endeavour to acquire strength of both mind and body.

Mary Wollstonecraft. *A Vindication of the Rights of Woman.* J. Johnson (1792).

Suffrage Organisations in the Early Twentieth Century

By the turn of the twentieth century, most members of Parliament were against the vote for women. Conservatives believed it would merely increase the number of votes received for the Liberals and the newly formed Independent Labour Party (ILP). The cause did receive some support from Liberal MPs, but many others, including Prime Minister Henry Campbell-Bannerman and his successor Herbert H. Asquith, opposed it. Members of the ILP, founded in 1892 to represent working men, also largely opposed women's suffrage as they believed that if property-owning women were granted the vote, the Liberals and Conservatives would gain a numerical advantage over them in elections. Many were supporters of universal suffrage, but some believed all men should get the vote first. The partisan objections to women's enfranchisement were not new and had been somewhat discreated by Barbara Bodichon decades earlier when the Reform Act of 1867 was being debated. She stated:

> In England, the extension proposed would interfere with
> no vested interests. It would involve no change in the
> principles on which our Government is based, but would
> rather make our Constitution more consistent with itself.
> Conservatives have a right to claim it as a Conservative
> measure. Liberals are bound to ask for it as a necessary
> part of radical reform. There is no reason for identifying

it with any class or party in the State, and it is, in fact, impossible to predict what influence it might have on party politics. The question is simply of a special legal disability, which must, sooner or later, be removed.

Barbara Bodichon. *Reasons for the Enfranchisement of Women*. National Association for the Promotion of Social Science (1866).

Even Queen Victoria had her say; a letter written to Prince Albert's biographer Sir Theodore Martin in 1870, stated:

The Queen is most anxious to enlist everyone who can speak or write to join in checking this mad, wicked folly of 'Women's Rights', with all its attendant horrors, on which her poor sex is bent, forgetting every sense of womanly feeling and propriety. God created men and women different, then let them remain each in their own position. Woman would become the most hateful, heartless, and disgusting of human beings were she allowed to unsex herself. And where would the protection be which man was intended to give to the weaker sex?

When people think of the suffrage movement in Britain today, they often recall the militant tactics employed by members of the WSPU. While their influence and importance on the movement cannot be overstated, other groups also made an impact on the fight for women's suffrage, not least of which was the NUWSS.

The National Union of Women Suffrage Societies

The National Union of Women's Suffrage Societies (NUWSS) was founded through the merger of the National Central Society for Women's Suffrage and the Central Committee of the National Society for Women's Suffrage and held its first meeting in November 1897 when Millicent

Garrett Fawcett was sworn in as its leader. The organisation was intended to unite the country's many suffrage societies with its mission stated as being, 'To obtain the parliamentary franchise on the same terms as it is, or may be, granted to men.' Primarily, its members were comprised of middle and upper-class people, although the number of working-class members would increase over time. Representatives from various trade unions, including textile workers, labourers, and women who worked for the mines, would discuss the movement with its leaders, and once persuaded of its merits would attempt to convince the women that they represented to join. Although the WSPU is much better known today, the NUWSS had a significantly larger membership. By 1914, there were nearly 500 suffrage societies allied to the NUWSS from all over the country, and the organisation boasted over 100,000 members, (today often referred to as suffragists), compared to only 2,000 members in the WSPU, (commonly known as suffragettes).

Fawcett labelled her own type of campaigning 'constitutional lobbying', and the WSPU's more militant way she called 'revolutionary lobbying'. The methods the NUWSS used to push for female suffrage included:

- Holding public meetings
- Organising petitions
- Writing letters and other communications with politicians
- Publishing their own newspaper, *The Common Cause*
- Distributing leaflets and other free literature
- Peaceful protests and marches.

On 11 November 1906, Fawcett held a banquet in the Savoy Hotel in honour of the suffragettes who were the first to go to prison and had just been released from Holloway. On the invitation, she put a statement that read:

> I need hardly say that I am convinced that the work of
> quiet persuasion and argument from the solid foundation

on which the success of the women's suffrage movement is reared: and I, in common with the great majority of suffrage workers, wish to continue the agitation on constitutional lines; yet we feel that the action of the prisoners has touched the imagination of the country in a manner which quieter methods did not succeed in doing. Many of us, therefore, desire to offer the prisoners some public mark of the value we attach to their self-sacrificing devotion.

Many women were members of both the NUWSS and the WSPU, and the two groups occasionally collaborated. On 9 February 1907, up to 4,000 women walked in a procession that stretched back half a mile. They headed for Hyde Park and then had a meeting in Exeter Hall in the Strand to call for votes for women. Although organised by the suffragists, many suffragettes were present despite the conditions being so bad that day that it became known as the 'Mud March'. While the two groups were willing to work together – and Fawcett praised the WSPU, saying they had revitalised the movement – there were some tensions. When the founder and leader of the Labour Party, Keir Hardie, spoke at the Mud March, some NUWSS members interrupted and hissed at him due to his connections with the suffragettes. He responded by saying that if the vote were won, it would be due to the actions of the 'suffragettes' fighting brigade.'

Many suffragists disliked the WSPU because they felt their tactics gave the suffrage movement a bad name. When criticised by anti-suffragists and some NUWSS members on her support of the WSPU, Fawcett pointed out that she did not support them when they were violent, but did when they were the victims of violence. It can also be argued that as WSPU militant activities increased, the number of individuals and societies that allied with the NUWSS continued to grow, suggesting that the publicity gained by the suffragettes' actions had a positive impact on increasing awareness of, and support for, the movement as a whole. In 1909, Fawcett wrote to Helena Dowson of the Nottingham branch of the NUWSS, stating that the rise in militant actions from the WSPU was deliberate and planned, as evidenced by articles in their magazine *Votes for Women,* and in the speeches of the suffragette leadership. She predicted that over time, the violence and criminal behaviour would escalate as it had done in the French Revolution and that this would put people off joining the WSPU.

Fawcett was initially a supporter of the Liberal Party, but as Labour was the only party that would not support a franchise bill that excluded all women, from 1912 she began giving Labour MPs some support (although she continued to support Liberal MPs who advocated for women's suffrage). When war broke out the political campaign of the NUWSS was suspended as it was deemed the correct course of action would be to utilise their organisational and money-raising skills to support the war effort. On 7 August 1914, Fawcett stated in *The Common Cause,* 'Let us show ourselves worthy of citizenship, whether our claim to it be recognised or not.' A year later, there was a split in the organisation with all its officers leaving, along with ten members of the executive committee, who were pacifists and believed that Britain should withdraw from the war. Fawcett remained the president of the NUWSS, as most of its grassroots members agreed that remaining patriotic and aiding in the war effort was the morally correct way to proceed.

The 1918 Representation of the People Act allowed some women to vote in the UK, and a year later, the National Union of Women Suffrage Societies became the National Union of Societies for Equal Citizenship. In the same year, Millicent Garrett Fawcett retired, and Eleanor Rathbone took over her duties. Rathbone was seen as the perfect replacement for Fawcett as she had been a leading campaigner for years and had previously been on the executive committee of the NUWSS. She had written many articles for *The Common Cause* and helped to unite the often politically and religiously fractured campaigners of her hometown when she co-founded the Liverpool Women's Citizens' Association in 1913, which educated women on political matters in preparation for the gaining of female enfranchisement.

A Brief Overview of the Women's Social and Political Union

After decades of trying to lobby and reason with Parliament to achieve female suffrage, some members of the NUWSS became disillusioned, believing more potent tactics were required to achieve their goals. On 10 October 1903, a meeting was held at Emmeline Pankhurst's home at 62 Nelson Street, Manchester, and the breakaway organisation, the Women's Social and Political Union, was formed. Mrs Pankhurst became the leader of the group, and along with close allies including her daughters Christabel, Sylvia and Adela, ushered in a new age of militant activism. The name was chosen because it demonstrated that it was a political rather than propagandist movement, and it showed an emphasis on achieving a more complete democratic society.

Their motto was 'Deeds, not words', and from the outset, they opposed any politician or political party that would not support their right to vote. While many men supported the WSPU and their mission, the organisation only permitted women to join, which made their militant tactics all the more sensational. Over the years, they demonstrated, marched, chained themselves to railings, accosted MPs and damaged property. Many were sent to prison for their actions, and hunger strikes were common among those who were. While their militancy did not immediately achieve their desired outcome, and may have even deterred people from supporting the organisation, it made significant strides in garnering publicity for the cause and attracted many more to the broader idea of women's suffrage. Many members of the WSPU gained notoriety and fame that would last for generations – though many more have been all but forgotten, despite greatly impacting society in their own time, and ours.

Other Suffrage Groups of the Early Twentieth Century

In Britain, small suffrage groups formed among workers or within local communities, though they would often be allied with the NUWSS, the WSPU or other organisations and usually more than one. Although there are too many to name here, some of the more prominent suffrage societies that were formed to fight for female suffrage in the early twentieth century included:

The International Alliance of Women for Suffrage (IAWS) – The IAWS was formed in 1902 and would later change its name to the International Women's Suffrage Alliance (IWSA). It allowed women from all over the world to share information, ideas and tactics on gaining suffrage, and meetings were held most years in a different country, starting in 1904 and continuing up to the outbreak of the First World War.

The Women's Freedom League (WFL) – The WFL was a group of women who broke away from the WSPU in 1907 as they sought a more democratic organisation than the one led by Emmeline Pankhurst and her daughter, Christabel. They believed in voting rights on the same terms as men, as did both the NUWSS and the WSPU, as well as most of the other smaller groups. While they were somewhat militant, they denounced violent tactics and preferred methods such as non-payment of taxes, not completing the mandatory census form, and chaining themselves to the gates of the Houses of Parliament. A journalist with *The Times* stated in October 1909 that the WFL had sixty-five branches across the country with around 5,000 members, and thousands more who sympathised with them. With the outbreak of the First World War, they suspended their protests and members were encouraged to engage in voluntary work. However, many were pacifists and refused to help the war effort at all, calling instead for a return to suffrage campaigning.

The Artist's Suffrage League (ASL) – The ASL was founded by Mary Lowndes in 1907 to help the NUWSS with the Mud March. Both for that protest and in subsequent years up to around 1918, they produced posters, Christmas cards, postcards and banners to help the propaganda campaign of the movement. Mary Lowndes contributed significantly to its artwork, along with other artists who were passionate about the cause, including Emily Ford, Barbara Forbes, Clara Billing, Dora Meeson Coates, Bertha Newcombe, and Emily J. Harding.

The Men's League for Women's Suffrage (MLWS) – The MLWS was founded in 1907 by a group of over forty left-wing intellectuals, including politicians, writers, journalists and barristers. They aimed to support the efforts of the NUWSS, and while they usually used non-militant tactics, they also endorsed the WSPU. They campaigned and lobbied for women to gain equal voting rights with men, although they were not a group affiliated with any particular political party. By 1910, the MLWS had ten branches across the country and much of their work was propaganda based, such as writing about the abuse faced by suffragettes while in prison.

The Actress's Franchise League (AFL) – The AFL was founded in 1908 by Gertrude Elliott, Adeline Bourne, Winifred Mayo and Sime Seruya, and was open not only to actresses but to any woman involved in the theatre. The main objectives of the organisation were to gain support within the theatrical industry for female enfranchisement, to work towards achieving the vote for women on the same terms as men, and to assist any other suffrage group as far as possible. As a whole, they neither supported nor condemned militant tactics, although some of their members were also members of the WSPU. They often held meetings where plays and skits were performed, and pro-suffrage literature was sold to raise funds. They also put on over 120 plays across the country between 1909 and 1914 to raise awareness about the cause and boasted over 900 members by 1914.

The Women Writers' Suffrage League (WWSL) – The WWSL was formed in 1908 by Cicely Hamilton and Bessie Hatton, both of whom were actresses and writers. They aimed to help bring about the vote for women through writing and allowed members from all walks of life, regardless of gender or political affiliation, as long as they had paid, published work. They often collaborated with the AFL, writing plays and other works for them to perform, and contributed to many suffrage publications of the day, including the NUWSS newspaper *The Common Cause*, and the WSPU publication *Votes for Women*. They were also active in demonstrations, although they tended to avoid the more politically charged protests, as their membership comprised supporters from all the main political parties.

The Church League for Women's Suffrage (CLWS) – The CLWS was founded by the Reverend Claude Hinscliff in 1909. CLWS member Edith Picton-Turbervill spoke on the subject of women's right to vote in a church in Ireland with permission from the Archbishop of Dublin, making her the first woman to preach in a Church of Ireland church (though the Irish church tended to shun the organisation because it would not denounce the militant actions of the WSPU). The main methods used to achieve their goals were prayer and education. However, in 1914, they revised their rules to allow members from across the country to participate in the activities of other suffrage groups. Emily Wilding Davison, who famously died under the King's horse at the Derby, was a member, and her funeral was attended by the group's founder, Claude Hinscliff. When some women were granted the vote in 1918, the CLWS believed it was not enough. In the following year, it was renamed The League of the Church Militants, which continued to fight for voting rights for women on the same terms as men.

The Women's Tax Resistance League (WTRL) – Dora Montefiore first proposed the formation of a tax resistance organisation in 1897. However, it was not until 1909 that the idea was brought to fruition with the establishment of the WTRL. They were associated with the Women's Freedom League, though many of their approximately 220 members, primarily middle-class, were also involved in other societies, both militant and constitutional. They aimed to withhold taxes until they were afforded the right to have a say on how those taxes were spent through voting rights. When bailiffs turned up to seize goods from members for sale at auction, they would demonstrate and gain publicity by giving speeches in public from decorated carriages to inform people why they were refusing to pay. With the outbreak of the First World War, it was decided that the patriotic thing to do was to suspend their protests, and most of the women of the WTRL began paying their taxes again.

The Men's Political Union for Women's Enfranchisement (MPU) – The MPU was founded in London in January 1910. They were one of the more militant, male-dominated groups within the women's suffrage movement, comprising of men from across the political spectrum. They worked closely with the WSPU and often put themselves between the suffragettes and the police or angry crowds of men at protests and other public gatherings. They were frequently subjected to police brutality, and when arrested and taken to prison, they would often take part in hunger strikes, inspired by their female counterparts.

The United Suffragists – The United Suffragists were founded in February 1914 as a breakaway group from the WSPU after founding members Emmeline Pethick-Lawrence and her husband Fred were ousted from the suffragette organisation as they did not approve of the group's increasing use of violence. Unlike the WSPU, men were permitted to join, as were non-militant suffrage campaigners. The suffragette newspaper *Votes for Women* was run by Emmeline and Fred, so it was now used by the new organisation instead. They continued to campaign throughout the war, attracting members from both the WSPU and the NUWSS, who disliked the truce called by the leadership of those groups. The United Suffragists, along with *Votes for Women*, was disbanded when the 1918 Representation of the People Act allowed some women over 30 to vote in the UK.

Teresa Billington-Greig – Founder of the Women's Freedom League

Teresa Billington (1876–1964) was born in Lancashire and grew up in Blackburn with her middle-class family. Her father was a shipping clerk and later worked for a company that manufactured boilers. Her maternal grandfather managed Preston's first department store, and her mother was the owner of a small business who ran a shop. Despite having little formal education, the young Teresa loved to read and to write, and had stories published in a Roman Catholic magazine. Her parents were very religious which was a cause of friction in the family, so at 17 years old Teresa ran away from home and was an outspoken agnostic throughout the rest of her life.

She became a teacher in Manchester after taking night classes but refused to teach religion to her students, which landed her in trouble with the Manchester Education Committee, most of whom wanted her to lose her job. However, one of their members was Emmeline Pankhurst and so impressed was she by Teresa that she arranged work for her in a Jewish school where she was not required to teach religion. Teresa joined the ILP and in 1903 became the party's organiser for Manchester, making her the first woman to hold the position. She used her station to advocate for equal pay for women in the workplace and subsequently became the secretary of the Manchester Equal Pay Committee. She joined the WSPU soon after its conception sometime in either late 1903 or early 1904 and began giving lectures at radical and unorthodox venues, such as ethical societies, trade unions, and Socialist Sunday Schools. In 1905, Keir

Hardie and Emmeline Pankhurst requested that she become a full-time organiser for the suffragette's activities with the Labour Party, and she became a paid employee of the WSPU in the following year.

She was sent to London to work with the prominent suffragette Annie Kenney, with whom she had demonstrated in the Royal Albert Hall in December 1905, and again at the House of Commons in April 1906. A month later she organised a demonstration in Trafalgar Square and was arrested on 21 June 1906 after leading a group of suffragettes to the Prime Minister's house. She was accused of hitting and kicking a police officer but claimed he had been aggressive with her first, causing her to have bruises and an inflamed throat. Despite witnesses confirming her claim, she was found guilty and ordered to pay a fine or serve a two-month prison sentence. She opted for the latter and became the first suffragette to serve a sentence in Holloway Prison. However, she was released soon after when an anonymous benefactor who had read about her in the *Daily Mirror* paid the fine (though this was against her wishes). In October of the same year, she served time again for two months after a demonstration at the opening of Parliament. Then she travelled back to Scotland upon her release, where she had previously been tasked with organising for the WSPU.

In 1907, Teresa married Frederick Lewis Greig in Glasgow, and the two adopted the double-barrelled surname, Billington-Greig. She was known affectionately as 'the woman with the dog whip', as she would wave a whip around her head to prevent others from ejecting her from political meetings she was interrupting. Fellow suffragette campaigner Helen Moyes wrote of her in *A Woman in a Man's World* (1971) 'The speaker who brought me to the militant movement was Theresa Billington-Greig. I can see her still, expounding logically, factually, forcefully and with telling illustrations of the need for women to vote.'

Emmeline Pankhurst and her daughters led the WSPU as a militant movement, believing that the leadership should be followed unquestioningly. In what was known as 'the split', the suffragettes had divided into two camps by September 1907, leading to the formation of the Women's Freedom League. Led by Teresa Billington-Greig, Charlotte Despard and Edith How-Martyn, they broke away from the autocratic WSPU as they believed that an organisation fighting for women's right to vote should be run democratically. The seventy or so women who joined the WFL, whose motto was 'Dare to be Free', ensured the organisation was run in a manner that allowed everyone's voice to be heard. While the WFL did engage in militant protests and took part in some of the events organised by the WSPU, often finding themselves on the wrong side of the law, they outright rejected acts of violence. An article probably written by Christabel Pankhurst in *Votes for Women* in October 1907 responded to the criticisms of the founding members of the breakaway group stating:

> If you have any pettiness of personal ambition, you must leave that behind before you come to this movement. There must be no conspiracies, no double dealing in our ranks. Everyone must fill her part. The founders and leaders of the movement must lead, the rank and file must loyalty share the burdens of the fight. For there is no compulsion to come into our ranks, but those who come must come as soldiers ready to march onwards in battle array.

In 1907, Billington-Greig debated Margaret Bondfield, a women's rights activist who was a member of the Adult Suffrage Society. Bondfield believed in universal adult suffrage for men and women alike, regardless of property ownership or wealth, but Billington-Greig argued that the aim of suffrage campaigners should be to obtain parliamentary franchise to women on the same terms as men as soon as possible. Bondfield argued that if this happened, not only would it give the Conservative Party a numerical advantage, but once middle-class women had the vote, many would stop fighting for the political interests of poorer women. She wished good luck to those fighting for suffrage on the same terms as men but followed it by saying that she objected to middle-class women claiming that they were fighting for the working classes. Billington-Greig won the vote that followed the debate by a margin of 171 to 139.

She became disillusioned with the WFL as its members were increasingly calling for a more violent approach so she left the organisation in 1910. At this point, she discontinued her activist work to focus instead on lectures and debates on women's suffrage, as well as other topics such as literary, philosophical, economic, political, feminist, ethical and rationalist issues, though the topic closest to her heart was female suffrage:

> I am a feminist, a rebel, and a suffragist – a believer, therefore, in sex-equality and militant action. I desire to see women free and human; I seek the complete emancipation from all shackles of law and custom, from all chains of sentiment and superstition.
>
> Teresa Billington-Greig. *The Militant Suffrage Movement*. F Palmer (1911).

Billington-Grieg became a journalist and wrote biographies of some of the women in the movement, as well as its general history. She also wrote articles criticising some of the policies of the WSPU. In a 1911 article titled 'Feminism and Politics' published in the *Contemporary Review*, she wrote, 'There is no feminist organisation and no feminist programme. And though the first is not essential, the second is.' She believed that the movement had become less of a rebellion and more of an 'emotional obsession', and that the leaders of the militants would be afraid of revolution if they did achieve it.

In another article, 'Militant Methods: An Alternate Policy', published in *The Fortnightly Review* in 1913, she stated that the 'Militant movement has kept to a straight, narrow way, and, lest it should touch life, it has cloaked itself with artifice and hypocrisy.' She recommended that, rather than attacking property as was standard at the time, they adopt a new approach. 'On one matter [a] protest could be made within the Police Court, on another outside, in public meetings, and in the public press … Strikes and boycotts could be employed on new feminist lines.'

During the war, she was involved in fundraising for various causes, including the 'Scottish Lassie' Motor Organisation Fund, which supported the Scottish Women's Hospitals for Foreign Service. In 1916, she organised events for the British Sportsmen's Ambulance Fund. She became a member of the Six Point Group, which was founded by Margaret Haig Thomas in 1921 and fought for six changes to the law aimed at bringing about a more equal society. She rejoined the WFL in 1937 and helped the organisation change its name to Women for Westminster in 1945, and then to merge with the National Women Citizens' Association three years later. Teresa Billington-Greig died of cancer in 1964 in the South London Hospital for Women.

Charlotte Despard – An All-Round Activist

Charlotte Despard (1844–1939) was one of seven children, six girls and one boy, and was born to a wealthy family in Kent. When she was 10 her father died and her mother was sent to an insane asylum, after which she lived with relatives in Edinburgh. A governess educated her and despite her privileged background, she always had a keen sense of what was just and unjust. In an unpublished memoir she stated that she had asked her teacher why God had made slaves, for which she was punished by being sent to bed. She was often jealous of the working-class children from a nearby village, believing them to be free because they did not have nurses and governesses to answer to. Not long after moving to Scotland, she tried to run away from home and catch a train to London. When that failed, she was isolated from her sisters for a few days before being sent away to boarding school.

She married the writer Maximilian Carden Despard in 1870 and began publishing novels herself soon after. Most were love stories but one, *A Voice from the Dim Millions*, was about the problems faced by a young factory worker, though she was unable to find a publisher for this book. After the death of her husband in 1890, she moved to Battersea in Wandsworth and dedicated herself to helping the area's poor by opening a soup kitchen for the unemployed, funding a health clinic and establishing youth clubs and working men's clubs. She also helped out on a committee tasked with reforming the Poor Laws, joined the Social Democratic Federation, and later became a member of the Independent Labour Party.

At some point, Despard joined the NUWSS but became frustrated with the slow progress of the constitutional suffragist movement, so in 1906 she joined the WSPU. In October that year, she was arrested during a protest at the House of Commons and in the following year, she was imprisoned twice more. Her brother, Sir John French, Inspector General of the British Army, was interviewed about his sister's involvement with the WSPU in the *Daily Mirror* on 15 February 1907. He stated, 'We have tried all we could to keep Mrs Despard from mixing up with these people … if she will join in this foolish agitation she must expect to suffer.' He believed authorities were too lenient on the suffragettes and that the WSPU was made up of women who were, 'All vain and some of them are a little mad. They get together and work themselves up into a state of bogus hunger for martyrdom.' Like others in the organisation, she came to believe that Emmeline and Christabel Pankhurst's stranglehold on decision-making within the WSPU was counterproductive. Along with Teresa Billington-Greig and Edith How-Martyn, she helped cause 'the split' of 1907 when together they formed the Women's Freedom League.

Despard's father had been Irish, and she spent a considerable amount of time campaigning in his homeland. While there in 1908 she helped Hanna Sheehy Skeffington and Margaret Cousins form the Irish Women's Franchise League (IWFL). Many Irish at the time wanted to break away from British rule and the IWFL campaigned to have a women's suffrage clause added to any proposed Home Rule Bill. Ireland had earlier women's suffrage groups such as the

Northern Ireland Society for Women's Suffrage formed in 1871, and the Dublin Women's Suffrage Association founded in 1876 (renamed the Irish Women's Suffrage and Local Government Association in 1901). The IWFL was the first to be built on the principles of militancy and, like the WSPU, they would use civil disobedience and sometimes violence to get their message across. While in Ireland, she also supported locked out workers during the labour dispute in Dublin and founded the Irish Workers' College in the same city.

She met with Mahatma Gandhi in 1909 and was influenced by his beliefs in passive resistance. Although she was happy to go to jail for the cause, she preferred non-violent methods of protest, such as having members chain themselves to the gate of the Lady's Gallery in the Palace of Westminster. She also advocated for non-payment of taxes, avoiding the 1911 census and attending non-militant marches such as the Women's Coronation Procession of 1911, which she led, and which involved many suffrage groups marching together in a show of peaceful solidarity. Despard also utilised her literary skills, regularly writing for the WFL's newspaper *The Vote*, alongside Teresa Billington-Greig and other talented writers, including Cicely Hamilton.

When war broke out, Despard, like many WFL members, refused to support the war effort due to her pacifist beliefs, despite her brother by this time holding the title Chief of Staff of the British Army and becoming the commander of the British Expeditionary Force sent to Europe in August 1914. She toured Britain speaking out against conscription and formed the pacifist organisation, the Women's Peace Crusade, which opposed all war. She also helped house refugee women and children, along with her long-time friend (and possibly her lover) Kate Harvey. Following the passing of the Parliament (Qualification of Women) Act of 1918, which granted women over 21 the right to stand for election as a Member of Parliament, Despard stood as the Labour Party candidate for Battersea in the General Election of the same year. She lost, and it is believed that this was due, at least in part, to her anti-war stance, which was extremely unpopular in the immediate aftermath of the Allied Powers' victory.

She would come into conflict with her brother again who was made Lord Lieutenant of Ireland in 1918 and was tasked with putting down the rebels who wanted Irish independence. Two years later, she collected evidence of atrocities committed by the army and the police in Cork and Kerry. She also helped form the Women's Prisoners' Defence League to support republican prisoners before becoming involved in the Sinn Féin campaign for a united Ireland. She was seen as a 'dangerous subversive' under the 1927 Public Safety Act by the Irish Free State Government as she opposed the Anglo-Irish Treaty (1921), and her house was continuously watched, being raided by authorities on more than one occasion.

Charlotte Despard's other notable activities include her avid involvement with the London Vegetarian Society from 1918, during which time she was also strongly opposed to cruelty to animals in all forms. She supported the Save the Children charity and was outspokenly in favour of the Indian independence movement. In 1930, she joined the Communist Party of Great Britain and was appointed secretary of the Friends of Soviet Russia organisation. She continued to campaign on several fronts well into her 90s and died on 10 November 1939, after a fall in her home near Belfast at the age of 95.

Dora Montefiore – The Suffrage Journeyman

Dorothy 'Dora' Frances Montefiore (1851–1933) was somewhat of a journeyman in the suffrage world and is an example of an activist who belonged to multiple organisations over the years, including some she helped establish and/or run. She came from a wealthy family and was the eighth of thirteen children born to Francis Fuller, a surveyor and railway entrepreneur, and his wife Mary Ann. Montefiore grew up in Surrey and was educated at home by tutors and governesses, and later attended a private school in Brighton. She described herself as having been a tomboy who was devoted to her father. He taught her to be curious and encouraged her to develop her intelligence, igniting a keen interest in people and society within her, he even had her help him prepare papers he would present to the British Association and Social Science Congresses.

In 1874, she married Australian businessman George Barrow Montefiore and moved to his homeland, where she bore two children. When he died in 1889, she was shocked to find how limited her guardianship over her own children was, as her husband had not stipulated in his will that she should be charged with caring for them. This sparked her interest in the issue of women's rights, seeing it as a righteous undertaking. She once stated:

> Surely it behoves those who are 'on the side of the Angels' to strive that woman's voice may be heard politically and socially in England and America, even as it is already heard in some of the Colonies of England, who in the first flush of young, inspired enthusiasm are leading their Motherland on the upward path.
>
> Dora Montefiore. *Why we Need Woman's Suffrage, and Why We Need It Now.* Shafts (1896).

She helped found the Women's Suffrage League of New South Wales, which held its first meeting at her home in 1891. The following year, she moved to Paris and later returned to London, where she became an executive member of the NUWSS. Montefiore became disheartened with the slow progress of gaining the vote for women, so along with her close friend Elizabeth Wolstenholme-Elmy, she joined the WSPU soon after it was formed. During the Boer War (1899–1902), she refused to pay income tax. She argued that, as a person ineligible to vote, she had no say in how much of her taxes would be spent on the military campaign, therefore it was not right that she should have to pay taxes. This resulted in bailiffs visiting her home in 1904 and 1905, seizing her goods and selling them to cover the cost of her taxes; however, she continued to refuse payment.

In May 1906, she orchestrated the 'Hammersmith Siege', barricading herself in her home to keep the bailiffs at bay, who again sought to seize her goods to settle her tax debts. She put up a banner that read, 'Women should vote for the laws they obey and the taxes they pay', and was assisted by other WSPU members, such as Annie Kenney and Teresa Billington-Greig. The newspapers dubbed her house 'The Fort' and 'Fort Suffragette' as members of the press, armed with cameras and notebooks, stalked the outside wall of the property trying to catch a glimpse of Montefiore. Some even attempted to scale the walls to enter the gardens but were thwarted by the police officers assigned to guard the house. She managed to keep her debtors out for six weeks, until they eventually gained entry and seized some of her household furniture.

She was a popular figure within the WSPU and regularly spoke for, and protested with, the group. She was arrested and sent to Holloway Prison alongside Adela Pankhurst and other suffragettes in October 1906 for 'using violent and abusive language' in a so-called attack on the House of Commons after they went to the lobby and caused a ruckus by loudly demanding votes for women. Despite her popularity, she became increasingly disillusioned with the leadership of the WSPU and its strong-arm tactics, which often involved violent protest. She also disliked the way decisions were being made and influenced by an elite few women while the rest of the members were supposed to follow along without question. As a result, Montefiore was a part of the group that broke away and formed the WFL in 1907. In the same year, she also joined the Adult Suffrage Society, and two years later became its honorary secretary. She was still adamant that, without parliamentary representation, women should not be required to pay taxes. In 1909, she helped establish the Women's Tax Resistance League to assist women who chose to protest by withholding taxes.

She was a skilled speaker and debater and wrote numerous articles on the subject of women's suffrage for journals, pamphlets and newspapers. Some of her most notable work included columns in *The New Age* between 1902 and 1906, as well as in the Social Democratic Federation's journal *Justice* between 1909 and 1910, along with articles in newspapers such as the *Daily Herald* and the *New York Call*. As a well-travelled person, Montefiore recognised that the issue of women's rights was an international one and she travelled the world lecturing on it. She spoke extensively throughout Europe and then undertook a tour of the USA in 1910 before returning to Australia, where she edited the newspaper, the *International Socialist Review of Australasia*. While there, she caused controversy by speaking out against compulsory military training for school-age boys. The following year, she was in South Africa for a brief period before returning to London. She soon caused even more controversy when she took 300 starving children from Dublin to England, leading to charges of kidnapping, although these charges would eventually be dropped. Dora Montefiore went on to become one of the early members of the Communist Party of Great Britain in 1920, alongside Sylvia Pankhurst. She published her autobiography, *From a Victorian to a Modern*, in 1927 and passed away on 21 December 1933, a day after her eighty-second birthday.

The Anti-Suffrage Movement

The anti-suffrage movement had gained momentum by the end of the 1880s in response to the increasing number of people campaigning for female suffrage. It was comprised of both men and women, as well as people from all social classes. In 1889, 104 women from the upper classes signed an appeal against granting the vote to women. Author Mrs Humphry Ward published the names in an article in the magazine *The Nineteenth Century*, and included in the list were Virginia Woolf's parents Julia and Leslie Stephen, and Helen Asquith, wife of the future Prime Minister Herbert. It is believed that one of the main reasons ladies from the higher orders did not want middle and lower-class women to vote was that they feared they might lose their place of privilege in society if too many radical changes to the law were brought in. Others believed that it would lead to neglect of the husband, which in turn would result in the total breakdown of the home, motherhood and ultimately the ruin of society. The fear was that if a man wanted, for example, to vote Conservative and his wife Liberal, it would cause significant problems in the home, a scenario that anti-suffrage campaigners envisioned would happen frequently should women gain the vote.

Another motive given by some from within the anti-suffrage movement was the perceived lower intelligence and lack of common sense of women. They argued that most women knew nothing about politics and, therefore, should not be allowed to vote. It can be argued that there was some truth to this viewpoint. In a debate in 1907, Frances Elinor Rendel from the Central Suffrage Society argued that this was because women had been excluded from politics and had not been educated on the subject. She urged women to educate themselves on the matter, stating that they should ask the men in their lives to teach them about politics so they could better fulfil their duty when women did eventually win the vote. This could be taken even further, as higher education was often less accessible to young women than it was to young men, especially those from the middle and upper classes. This had nothing to do with intellectual potential, however, and as Rendel alluded to, if (and when) women were given the same level of education, they had the same potential intellect as men.

In July 1908, the Women's National Anti-Suffrage League (WNASL) was formed by novelist and educator Mary Humphrey Ward at the behest of Lord George Nathaniel Curzon, and MP Sir William Randal Cremer. The WNASL aimed to counter the growth of the WSPU and represent the many women who did not support women's suffrage. Ward objected to women voting in elections and becoming MPs, believing that constitutional, legal, financial, military and international problems should be left for men to solve. She did, however, feel that women should be involved in policymaking within local bodies, as they may possess expert knowledge on domestic and social matters about the local community. Over a hundred branches were formed throughout its existence, which published leaflets in conjunction with the *Anti-Suffrage Review*. They managed to gather hundreds of thousands of signatures from people who, like them, opposed the suffrage movement, and they received praise for their work from Prime Minister Herbert H. Asquith.

The WNASL's badge depicted a woman reading to her two children, a boy and a girl, which was symbolic of the belief that a woman's primary role was as a mother and a wife. Meanwhile, posters and other propaganda put out by the anti-suffrage campaign suggested that women were too much ruled by emotion to be allowed to vote, and it was believed that menstruation and childbirth also debilitated them to the point of making the chance to vote unrealistic. The WNASL lasted two years before merging with the Men's League for Opposing Woman Suffrage, which had been formed in 1909. Together they became the National League for Opposing Woman Suffrage, which allowed members from both sexes. The organisation continued campaigning along the same lines, opposing the efforts of both suffragettes and suffragists right up to the passing of the Representation of the People Act in 1918.

Sir Almroth Edward Wright, an eminent bacteriologist and immunologist, was one of the most outspoken members of the anti-suffrage movement. In a letter to *The Times* on 2 March 1912, he expressed the view that female suffrage would damage both the country and the Empire as women were physically, intellectually and morally inferior to men. He believed both the suffragettes and the suffragists suffered from sexual frustration, which manifested in their protests for what he believed to be preposterous goals, such as the vote and equal pay for equal work.

> But now with the new century has come to fruition a new
> thing, and colour has a fresh significance. What is the new

thing? Political societies started by women, managed by women and sustained by women. In their dire necessity they have been started; with their household wit they manage them; in their poverty, with ingenuity and many labours, they sustain them. The men look on. Are their eyes holden, or do they begin to see that in all the stresses and strains is a hint of new treasures to be added to the national life.

> Mary Lowndes. *Banners and Banner Making*. The Artist's Suffrage League (1909).

CHAPTER THREE

Suffrage Propaganda and the Battle for Hearts and Minds

The fight for female suffrage was considered old news by 1905 and much of the media had lost interest. Meetings were ignored by the press and they usually refused to publish letters and articles sent in by campaigners. At this time, the majority of the British public were still opposed to female suffrage, so the various suffrage groups raised their propaganda efforts in a bid to convey the message and win the battle for hearts and minds. However, the anti-suffrage movement was not far behind with its own attempts at propaganda aimed at persuading the general populace that they were right in their conviction that only men should be permitted to vote. Posters, postcards, artwork and writing would all play a part in this publicity war, but it was arguably the militant actions of the WSPU that were most effective as they regularly made headline news, directly catching the public's attention and bringing awareness to the cause for women's suffrage.

The First Militant Protest of the WSPU

On 13 October 1905, Annie Kenney joined forces with Christabel Pankhurst and participated in the first militant protest of the WSPU. The two attended a meeting at the Manchester Free Trade Hall where they heckled Liberal politicians, shouting, 'Will the Liberal Government give votes to women?' The idea was that it was time for militant action if they refused to give a straight answer and before setting off from the Pankhurst home at Nelson Street, Christabel predicted the outcome and told her mother, 'We shall sleep in prison tonight.' When Kenney asked the question, as predicted, she was ignored. When the chairman of the meeting tried to continue on with proceedings, she stood up again but was manhandled by two men next to her in the audience. After managing to unfurl their banner, which read, 'Will You Give Votes for Women?' they were forcibly ejected from the venue.

As other audience members left the hall after the meeting, Kenney attempted to make a speech but was dragged away by the police, making her the first suffragette to be arrested for the cause. Christabel wanted to be taken into custody, too, but needed to do something to make this happen. Unable to assault a policeman as he was holding her arms, she spat at the officer and then at a bystander who she also reportedly struck in the mouth, which was enough to get her arrested for technical assault. The prosecuting solicitor stated that they acted like 'women of the slums', though according to the *Manchester Guardian* reporting on the 16 October 1905, Christabel claimed when addressing the bench:

> I want to explain as clearly as I can that at the time I committed the assault that is complained of I was not aware that the individuals assaulted were police officers. I thought they were Liberals … My conduct in the Free Trade Hall was meant as a protest against the legal position of women today. We have no vote; and so long as we have not votes we must be disorderly.

When the magistrates retired to consider the verdict, the defendants unfurled a banner in the dock that read 'Votes for Women', though it was removed from the court before sentence was passed. Both women could pay a fine for their actions, but they refused and opted for prison. Kenney received three days in Strangways, and as the senior figure, Christabel received seven days. Their incarceration made headlines and became worldwide news, gaining significant support for the organisation in the process. It was also the first time the words 'Votes for Women' were used on a placard, marking the creation of one of the most memorable and important political slogans in British history.

Upon Christabel's release, a large crowd greeted her, then followed her to the Free Trade Hall where both ladies spoke, though neither discussed their time in prison instead opting to focus on the movement's future. It can be argued that with this first militant action and the ensuing arrests, the WSPU became genuinely distinct from the NUWSS and other suffrage organisations, and the sentiment of their motto, 'Deeds Not Words' was first truly manifest.

Suffragette Propaganda and the Press

On 10 January 1906, a few months after the arrests of Annie Kenney and Christabel Pankhurst, *Daily Mail* journalist Charles Hands coined the term 'suffragette' to describe WSPU members. It was intended to be an insult as the 'ette' made them sound small and like a feminine imitation of the real thing. Not to be outdone, the WSPU leadership turned this on its head and pronounced it with a hard 'g' to sound like 'suffra get', emphasising their belief that they would *get* the vote. Today, the term suffragette is synonymous with the organisation's members. It is used to distinguish militant suffrage campaigners from their constitutional counterparts, particularly in the NUWSS, who are commonly known as suffragists (though the press of the early twentieth century would usually continue to use the term suffragist to describe all suffrage activists).

A week later, Bernard Partridge published a cartoon in *Punch*, a satirical magazine aimed at the educated middle classes. It depicted a 'shrieking sister' being talked down to by a suffragist who says, 'You Help Our Cause? Why, You're Its Worst Enemy.' The Liberal publication generally favoured women's suffrage and was described by Millicent Garrett Fawcett as having been 'faithful friends' of the suffrage movement. However, like many other publications and individuals, it supported the concept of female franchise but opposed the militant actions of the WSPU.

Sometimes even the same newspaper would argue for both sides. On 12 February 1907 the WSPU staged a protest opposite the Houses of Parliament as the King's speech failed to mention women's suffrage. A melee ensued between police and suffragettes that lasted three hours and when the *Daily Mirror* reported the scene a couple of days later, they stated that desperate suffragettes were rioting and attacking police with their umbrellas. The paper described the scene in a critical way towards WSPU members, saying, 'Something like pandemonium ensued. The women began to fight like tigers, and they received and inflicted many bruises.' After a court hearing the next day, on 15 February the *Daily Mirror* changed its tune. The article printed that day reported on the police brutality faced by the suffragettes and said that they had been kicked, struck, and trampled by police horses. It even went as far as to suggest the WSPU were winning, pointing out that they had made authorities so nervous that women now had to be accompanied by an MP when they visited Parliament, who would be responsible for their good conduct.

The 'Women's Parliament' demonstrations were events that took place at the start of each Parliament, when WSPU members would march on the House of Commons to attempt to deliver a petition to the Prime Minister. The first took place on 19 February 1906, where Emmeline Pankhurst, Dora Montefiore and Annie Kenney addressed the 300–400 women who attended. Mrs Pankhurst later stated that although at the start of that day she was still upset at the snub of the King's speech, seeing the crowds march with her gave her great hope for the future.

> Out of the disappointment and dejection of that experience,
> I yet reaped a richer harvest of happiness than I had ever
> known before. Those women had followed me to the

House of Commons. They had defied the police. They were awake at last. They were prepared to do something that women had never done before – fight for themselves. Women had always fought for men, and for their children. Now they were ready to fight for their own human rights. Our militant movement was established.

Emmeline Pankhurst. My Own Story.
London Eveleigh Nash (1914).

By the end of 1906, Emmeline Pethick-Lawrence, the financial strategist for the WSPU, was running the organisation on the equivalent of £10,000 per week in today's money, which incorporated salaries for eight women including Annie Kenney, Minnie Baldock and Christabel Pankhurst who were in charge of the London branch. The money came from donations from wealthy supporters, sales of materials such as books, postcards and pamphlets, and subscriptions from the fifty-eight branches that had sprung up nationwide in that year. They saved money by not spending on advertising, instead, they wrote what they needed to convey in chalk on buildings and pavements. They also saved by not hiring halls and instead, they held street meetings or gathered in other public places such as parks and stood on boxes or chairs to make their speeches.

Sometimes raising money took creative thinking and ingenuity. To finance the 'monster meeting' that would be known as 'Women's Sunday' and was to be held at Hyde Park on 21 June 1908, Emmeline Pethick-Lawrence had a 'self-denial' week in February whereby WSPU members were asked to do without something for a week and donate the money they saved to the WSPU funds. This could be anything from a pair of stockings to afternoon tea with friends, and the idea proved so successful that it became an annual event.

At the South Aberdeen by-elections in February 1907, the Liberal candidate's majority was slashed from 4,000 to 400, despite Aberdeen being a major stronghold for Scottish Liberals. This was partly due to suffragette campaigning against the Liberal Party. Some local newspapers were sympathetic to the WSPU, and the *Aberdeen Free Press* believed that their involvement in the loss of support for the Liberals demonstrated the movement was led by women of culture, high character, and intense moral earnestness. A WSPU branch was opened in the city soon after by Caroline Philips, a journalist for the *Aberdeen Daily Journal*.

At the Women's Parliament on 20 March 1907, Annie Kenney led a group of 300 women dressed as mill girls. At first, they were mistaken for onlookers and managed to make progress on a street towards the Parliament buildings but soon found themselves fighting a group of police officers. The next day, the *Daily Mirror* described them as 'Mill Girl Amazons' who struggled 'manfully' with the police despite the clogs they wore, causing them to slip on the pavement.

On 30 June 1908, twelve suffragettes arrived at the House of Commons and requested to speak with the Prime Minister. When he refused, they left and returned in the early evening with megaphones, beseeching the crowd to help them gain access to Parliament. According to *The Times*, the crowd that gathered was not there to support the suffragettes but to witness the commotion. When they tried to get past police officers, there was what *The Times* called the 'fiercest scrimmage' with a leader from the mob made up of 'hooligans' pushing the ladies further towards their intended destination. The police held firm, however, and the women were arrested and taken to Canon Row Police Station. Twenty-seven women were arrested and received sentences ranging from one to three months in prison.

Another strategy used by the WSPU to good effect was finding out where a particular politician would be, then shouting at them and generally harassing them. They frequently questioned Asquith and his cabinet members about votes for women outside their homes or other locations, hammering home the point that they would never give up, and as their attempts to talk to the MPs were cheeky and often comical, they attracted much attention from onlookers and the press.

The first edition of the suffragette newspaper *Votes for Women* was published in the first week of October 1907 with the first editorial called *The Battle Cry*. This militaristic, along with religious language, would become a regular part of suffragette propaganda, they adopted Joan of Arc as their patron saint, and some would dress in medieval armour in her honour at their processions. The first issue was dedicated not only to women fighting for freedoms but 'To all women all over the world, of whatever race, creed, or calling, whether they be with us or against us in this fight.'

The paper, which was a monthly publication at first but would be published every week from April 1908, wrote about unjust laws and encouraged solidarity with feminists not just in the UK, but across the globe. The importance of *Votes for Women* in the propaganda campaign of the WSPU cannot be overstated. It sold around 30,000 copies in 1909, which rose to around 40,000 in 1910 but the readership was probably much higher as the newspapers would be passed around among friendship groups and work colleagues. In her unpublished memoirs Kitty Marion stated:

> One of the first things I learned [after joining the WSPU] was to sell the paper *Votes for Women* on the street. That was the 'acid' test. All new recruits who were anxious to 'do something' were told the best thing they could do was to take a bundle of papers and show the 'faith that was in them' by standing on the street with it, even if they didn't sell any, as long as they held up *Votes for Women* to the public and advertised the cause.
>
> Kitty Marion. *Papers of Kitty Marion*.
> The Women's Library (*c.* 1908–1933).

Fred and Emmeline Pethick-Lawrence edited and funded *Votes for Women* and were close friends of Emmeline Pankhurst. Mrs Pethick-Lawrence was a high-ranking member of the WSPU and not only helped fund the organisation, but was innovative with her ideas, such as coming up with the colour scheme that would be adopted by the suffragettes, which consisted of:

- Purple – The colour of royalty, signifying the dignity of the ladies in the movement.
- White – Representing the purity of the suffragettes' motives.
- Green – The symbol of spring, which represented hope.

On Women's Sunday, over 300,000 people attended, with more than 30,000 of them directly involved in the march, likely making it the largest demonstration in the UK up to that date. It was intended to encourage the Liberal Government to support the cause, and, in the build-up, fifteen rooms were rented nearby to prepare handbills, postcards and pamphlets to be distributed during the event. Thousands of copies of *Votes for Women* were ready for sale, and £1,000 was spent on hoardings to be placed in London and other major cities, featuring posters of the women who would be speaking at the twenty platforms available on the day. Advertising the event was also done via pavement chalking, door-to-door canvasing, and ladies walking up and down busy streets with flyers and wearing sandwich boards. In the days after Women's Sunday, several newspapers reported positively on the event, including *The Daily Mail, The Daily Express,* and *The Standard.* They talked about the peaceful demeanour of the speakers and the vast crowd that had come to see them. According to *The Times*, 'The demonstration organisers had counted on an attendance of 250,000 ... Probably it was double, and it would be difficult to contradict anyone who asserted confidently that it was trebled.'

However, not everyone who turned up to watch the suffragettes speak at these types of events was in support of them. In the summer of 1908, when members of the WSPU spoke at open-air meetings, a music-hall song called *Put Me Upon an Island Where the Girls Are Few* would often be sung by onlookers who opposed them. A song like this would be easy to remember and its mocking tones may even have influenced some people's beliefs against them. The chorus of the song was as follows:

> Put me upon an island where the girls are few,
> Put me among the most ferocious lions in the zoo,
> You can put me up on a treadmill and I'll never, never fret,
> But for pity sake don't put me near a suf-fra-gette!

WSPU members were always trying to find new and novel ways to get the message out. On 17 February 1909 the *Daily Express* reported in an article called 'Suffragist in an Airship':

> The suffragists, not content with their infantry assaults, cavalry parades, motor and char-a-banc demonstrations, and steamboat trips, took to the air yesterday. At least, Miss Muriel Matters, one of their youngest but more determined warriors did … The Government knows a good deal about dropping Bills already, but Miss Matters taught them still another way – how to drop them from an airship.

The Pethick-Lawrences organised the 'Woman's Exhibition and Sale of Work in the Colours' in London in May 1909, where goods made in the colours of purple, white and green were sold to raise money for the WSPU. Sylvia Pankhurst and a group of art students created murals containing symbolic imagery, tea was served in sets made up of suffragette colours, and fifty stalls sold various items, including food, sweets, clothing and jewellery. There was even a new model bicycle painted in WSPU colours and sporting a badge designed by Sylvia featuring an angel on tiptoes standing at a signpost for freedom. The two-week-long exhibition raised a total of £5,664, and according to Mrs Pethick-Lawrence, the WSPU gained 150 new members.

Suffragette merchandise first became available during the Christmas season of 1907, and once retailers saw the potential for sales, stores began stocking items in suffrage colours. The most famous to do so was Selfridges, which sold clothes, fashion accessories, tea, cigarettes and chocolate bars with the words 'Votes for Women' imprinted on them. On 31 December 1909, Selfridges placed a quarter-page advertisement in *Votes for Women* promoting new products linked to the WSPU, including notepaper, envelopes, diaries, gloves and wrist bags, all made in suffragette colours and/or featuring slogans that showed support for the cause.

The WSPU also had their own stores. In 1908, Annie Kenney opened a shop at 37 Queen's Road, Clifton, open daily from 10 am to 7 pm. Others were opened in London, Liverpool, Leicester, Newcastle and Bath around the same time. These shops maintained a permanent presence in a prime location making them visible to the public and their windows served as advertising space for upcoming events. The shops sold merchandise, campaign literature, jams, cakes and preserves made by members and meetings would often be held in a back or upstairs room, saving money on hiring places. There was a downside to owning their own stores however, because when the WSPU began smashing windows, some of their shops – particularly in Newcastle and Bristol – were targeted by anti-suffrage locals who smashed their windows in retaliation. The popularity of merchandise made in suffragette colours would continue to grow until 1912, when increased militancy meant that members would no longer be keen to wear the colours and advertise their membership as they preferred to avoid police attention.

Picture postcards were another popular tool in the propaganda campaigns of the women's suffrage movement though the anti-suffrage movement also employed them. They were invented in the late nineteenth century and were seen as a valuable means of conveying a message. Postcards produced by the anti-suffrage movement often suggest that if women were granted political power, traditional roles in the home would break down. They showed men having to do housework, cooking and looking after the children, and suggested this would result in chaos. Suffrage campaigners are often pictured as grotesque as a means of indicating that they are abnormal, and that any 'normal' woman looking at the card should shun them and their movement. Postcards were helpful as they could be used for non-political purposes and were sent by people to convey simple messages, such as the stereotypical 'Wish you were here'. Someone receiving the card may not be aligned with one side or the other, so the images could plant a seed in the reader that female suffrage was either good or bad, depending on who created it.

Flora Drummond – The General

Some of the movement's more colourful characters were so newsworthy that their mere presence was an aid to the propaganda campaign; foremost among these was Flora Drummond (1878–1949). Her affectionate nickname was 'the General' because she would wear a military-style uniform with an officer's cap and epaulettes while marching with the suffragettes and would often be seen leading processions while riding a large horse. She was born in Manchester but had family roots on the Isle of Arran in Scotland, where she spent much of her childhood. As a young adult, she trained to become a postmistress but missed out because at 5ft 1in tall, she was an inch shorter than the height requirement for the post. She was then trained in shorthand and typing, and after marrying Joseph Drummond in 1898 she moved back to Manchester with him, where he was employed as an upholsterer.

When he lost his job she became the family's primary breadwinner, working as a manager at the British Oliver Typewriter Company factory, where she first experienced the poor working conditions faced by her fellow working-class women, some of whom were forced into using prostitution to supplement their low income. Drummond joined the Fabian Society and the ILP in Manchester and witnessed the arrest of Christabel Pankhurst and Annie Kenney in 1906 at the Liberal Party election meeting at the Free Trade Hall in Manchester. When the two were released from prison, she attended a celebratory rally where she was persuaded to join the WSPU. Soon after, she relocated to London which by this time was the centre of suffrage activity.

She was known for her courageous stunts that grabbed headlines, the first of which was sneaking inside the House of Commons at the end of 1906 which led to her serving the first of nine stints in Holloway Prison. She also once snuck into 10 Downing Street, taking advantage of the distraction caused by the arrest of her friend Irene Miller who had knocked on the door. In another of her more famous exploits she hired a boat, approached the Palace of Westminster from the River Thames and used a megaphone to shout at MPs sitting on the riverside terrace. *The Times* wrote of the incident on 19 June:

> The woman suffragists, whose Great Hyde Park demonstration on Sunday next is rousing the attention of all London, yesterday made one of the most dramatic moves of their campaign. With fine generalship the suffragists advanced on the Terrace … Several hundred MPs, Pan-Anglican clerks, constituents, and a host of delightfully dressed women friends sat in the cool shade …
>
> The steam launch came nearer. A band played merrily on the deck … High over it was hoisted a large white banner with an announcement of Sunday's demonstration Abaft was another banner with the inscription: 'Cabinet Ministers especially invited.' As the launch drew alongside Mrs Drummond stood up on the cabin roof and, waving her arms, began to harangue the astounded MPs who had always fancied that on the Terrace they were safe from suffragist attacks.

Drummond became a paid organiser in 1908, working out of the WSPU headquarters in Clement's Inn. She was skilled in administration, excelled at organising and leading demonstrations, and was an excellent public speaker with a knack for putting hecklers in their place with her witty comebacks. When Mary Phillips was released from prison after serving three months in Glasgow, Drummond organised a welcome home committee. They all wore tartan sashes and were entertained by the General playing the bagpipes, who later told the press that their struggle was comparable to that of William Wallace. Although the idea of women chaining themselves to railings has become an image strongly associated with the movement, it was a relatively rare event – though that did not stop Drummond being involved in an example of it. The *Daily Express* reported on 18 January 1908:

> The militant women suffragists made another raid on No. 10 Downing Street … Two of their number, Mrs Drummond and Miss Mary Garth, succeeded in reaching the swing doors leading to the historic council chamber. While these women were being ejected two others, Miss [Edith] New and Nurse Chew [Olivia Smith], chained and padlocked themselves to the railings outside the premier's residence … 'Votes for women!' Shouted the two voluntary prisoners simultaneously, 'Votes for women!'

She was sentenced to three months, along with Emmeline and Christabel Pankhurst, for attempting to rush the House of Commons during a protest in Trafalgar Square later in 1908. She was given the option of the sentence being bound over but despite being pregnant at the time she chose prison. After fainting, she was released early and as she left, Mrs Pankhurst shouted, 'I am glad because now you will be able to carry on the work.' When born, her son was named Keir Hardie Drummond in honour of the Labour Party founder and leader. In 1909, Mrs Pankhurst laid down the gauntlet when an edition of *Votes for Women* stated, 'Beautiful, haughty, dignified, stern Edinburgh, with your cautious, steadfast people, you have not yet woken up to take part in our militant methods.' Drummond responded to this by organising the first militant procession the city would see, which took place in October of that year. The procession was watched by tens of thousands of people and featured women playing the bagpipes while others carried banners with pro-suffrage slogans written on them. Many were dressed in their working clothes, while others marched dressed as inspirational women from Scotland's past.

During her multiple stays in Holloway Prison, she endured frequent hunger strikes and force-feeding and although she was always willing to participate in these demonstrations, they took a toll on her health. Consequently, in 1914, she returned to the Isle of Arran to recuperate and when she returned to London, she focused on public speaking and administrative work. With the outbreak of the First World War, she helped with the WSPU's recruitment efforts and when some women were granted the vote in 1918, she was an essential part of Christabel Pankhurst's campaign to become a Member of Parliament. She continued to fight for women's rights and remained an integral part of the movement for voting rights on the same terms as men until it was achieved with the Equal Franchise Act of 1928, having had the honour less than a month earlier of being a pallbearer at the funeral of Emmeline Pankhurst. Flora Drummond lived out her last years in Arran after the death in 1944 of her second husband, Alan Simpson. She died in 1949, aged 70.

Sarah Jane Baines – The First Suffragette to Face Trial by Jury

Sarah Jane Baines (1866–1951), commonly known as Jennie Baines, was the daughter of James Edward Hunt and Sarah Ann Hunt. She was born in Birmingham and left school aged 11 to work with her parents at an ordnance factory owned by statesman Joseph Chamberlain. At the age of 14, she joined the Salvation Army, an organisation that believed in equality between the sexes, and soon rose up the ranks, gaining a reputation as an excellent public speaker. She helped women who had been arrested and was arrested herself for her anti-establishment speeches on behalf of the Salvation Army. She married

George Baines in 1888, and over the next decade she bore him five children, though only three of them would survive childhood. In addition to motherhood, she worked as a sewing machinist during this time, yet she maintained her political spirit, joining the ILP and actively participating in the temperance movement. She also sat on a committee tasked with feeding school children and was a member of the unemployed committee.

She heard Emmeline Pankhurst speak in 1903 and was impressed, but it was after reading about Annie Kenney and Christabel Pankhurst becoming the first suffragettes to be arrested for the cause in 1905 that she was prompted to join the WSPU. Baines was arrested on 13 December 1906 and sentenced to fourteen days in prison. While there, her concern for imprisoned women was reinforced, and she claimed that this experience made her more rebellious than ever. By February 1908, she was made a paid organiser of the WSPU and became an integral part of the movement, organising open-air rallies, disrupting political meetings and establishing new branches of the WSPU in the North of England and the Midlands. She was also invited to speak at Women's Sunday at Hyde Park on 21 June 1908, alongside other paid members such as Emmeline and Christabel Pankhurst, Emmeline Pethick-Lawrence, Annie Kenney and Flora Drummond.

She helped grab the headlines in November 1908, when, as Herbert H. Asquith left a railway station in Leeds, Baines and a group of suffragettes were there to meet him. According to the 26 November 1908 issue of *Votes for Women*, she yelled at him 'Votes for Women and down with tyranny!' She then led a march to the venue where he was due to speak and shouted, 'If these tyrants refuse to listen to us break down the barriers, break down the doors, and compel a hearing.' Baines joined up with Alfred Kitson, who was leading a group of unemployed people from Leeds in a separate protest, and the two were charged with causing a riot. When her trial took place, she made the newspapers again when she became the first suffragette to be tried by a jury. She was defended by Fred Pethick-Lawrence and refused to recognise the authority of an all-male jury as she did not consider them her peers. She was found guilty of unlawful assembly at the Coliseum in Leeds and was sentenced to serve six weeks in Armley Gaol.

Jennie Baines was arrested fifteen times and went on hunger strike five times, which would result in her almost immediate release due to her suffering from a condition known as chorea or 'St Vitus' dance,' which caused uncontrolled spasms which could be brought on by emotional stress. Her most notorious piece of activism was in July 1912 when, along with Mary Leigh, Gladys Evens and Mabel Capper, Baines (using the name Lizzie Baker) took part in the attempt to burn down the Theatre Royal in Dublin. She received seven months' hard labour but was released after five days as a result of her hunger strike.

On 8 July 1913, she went with her husband and her son, who was 16 at the time, and blew up an empty railway carriage. When police searched their home, they found a bomb, a loaded handgun, black masks, various tools and two catapults. Her husband George and their son were released on bail, but Jennie was sent to prison. She again went on a hunger strike and was released soon after, but her health suffered so much that her doctor told her she would likely die if she were to go without food again. It was determined that a move away from Britain would be prudent, so in December 1913, Baines and her family escaped to Australia. She continued her activism and soon began work for the Women's Political Association and the Victorian Socialist Party.

When the First World War broke out, she opposed the pro-war stance taken by the WSPU and stayed in Australia where she campaigned against conscription in 1916. The following year, she led a series of militant protests organised by the Women's Peace League against the surging cost of living, accusing the Australian Government of profiteering from the war. She was imprisoned then released on appeal but was sent to prison again in 1919 for flying a prohibited communist flag. This time, she was sentenced to six months but was released soon after because, despite her ill health, she went on a hunger strike again, becoming the first prisoner in Australia to do so.

She stated in an article that appeared in *The Socialist* on 11 April 1919, 'To fight for that which is better and nobler in this world is to live in the highest sense, but to submit and tolerate the evils which exist is to merely vegetate in the sewers of iniquity.' She helped form the Victorian branch of the Communist Party of Australia in 1920 along with Adela Pankhurst but was expelled five years later as she disagreed with some of the polices of Joseph Stalin. She rejoined the Labour Party and went on to become a special magistrate to the South Melbourne Children's Court from 1928 to 1948. Jennie Baines continued to fight for the causes she believed in for the rest of her life; she died of cancer aged 84 in Port Melbourne on 20 February 1951.

Daisy Solomon and Elspeth McClelland – The Human Letters

Daisy Dorothea Solomon (1882–1978) was born in Cape Town to a South African father, Saul Solomon and a Scottish mother, Georgiana Margaret Solomon. She grew up surrounded by radical beliefs as her father was in favour of a multi-racial government and advocated for women's rights, and her mother was a suffrage campaigner. The family moved to Scotland in 1888, and after Saul's death a few years later, they settled in Hampstead, London. Solomon, along with her mother, joined the Women's Liberal Association, but by 1908 they had decided that a more militant form of activism was needed, and so joined the WSPU. Less is known about Elspeth Douglas McClelland (1879–1920), who was raised in Yorkshire by her accountant father John McClelland, and her mother Epsey McClelland. Elspeth was an architect by trade and was probably the only female among 600 students at the Polytechnic Architectural School in London.

When the Prime Minister would not hear a delegation of women to discuss female suffrage, the WSPU decided to take matters into their own hands and take advantage of the Post Office regulation that allowed people to be 'posted' by express delivery. On 23 February 1909, Jessie Kenney, (sister of Annie Kenney), took Solomon and

McClelland to the East Strand Post Office. There, they purchased a three-penny stamp, and the pair were addressed to 'The Right Hon H.H. Asquith, 10 Downing Street, SW.' When they paid for the stamp, neither was carrying a placard, but by the time they were taken by a telegram messenger, they were both carrying boards advertising a deputation that was planned for the following day.

They were 'delivered' by a messenger to the front door and were accompanied by Christabel Pankhurst and Flora Drummond, but the stunt was curtailed when an official came out. According to the *Daily Mirror* published the day after, the Downing Street representative said, 'You cannot be delivered here. You must be returned; you are dead letters.' It was pointed out that the addressee, the Prime Minister, had no obligation to accept the delivery hence their status as 'dead letters', meaning letters that could not be delivered. The two ladies protested that they had been paid for, but were returned to the WSPU offices at Clement's Inn. Asquith, who was often at odds with the suffragettes, saw the humorous side of the unique protest, which, as intended, was widely reported and made front-page news in the *Daily Mirror*.

The London Post Office put out a statement after the 'human letters' incident stating that any other women attempting to be posted to prominent politicians or places of political importance should be refused, but a similar incident did occur on 11 September 1912 in Scotland. Winston Churchill was to give a speech in Dundee and suffragette Lila Clunas was turned away. Undeterred, she put a postal card addressed to Churchill at his residence and, like Solomon and McClelland a few years earlier, requested that it be delivered by express mail. When she got there, she was also refused an audience, being told that the MP was not at home to callers.

The day after their attempted express delivery, Solomon and McClelland were cheered when they attended the Women's Parliament meeting at Caxton Hall. At the end of the meeting, Solomon joined a delegation to approach Asquith and was one of twenty-eight suffragettes arrested. This was her first arrest, and like many others, she went on a hunger strike and was force-fed.

The delegation generated national and even international headlines as some of those arrested, including Solomon, Constance Lytton and Emmeline Pethick-Lawrence, were upper-class ladies.

Elspeth McClelland married William Albert Spencer in 1912. They had three children together, but she died giving birth in 1920. Daisy Solomon served as the joint branch secretary of the WSPU Hampstead branch from 1912 to 1913. By 1915, she was the joint secretary of the United Suffragists, a breakaway group from the WSPU, and after the First World War, she continued to fight for votes on the same terms as men. Once that was achieved in 1928, she continued to campaign for women's rights in both Britain and South Africa and died in her mid-nineties in 1978.

The Cambridge University Library Suffrage Posters

Marion Phillips was an active member of the women's movement who served as an MP for the Labour Party from 1929 to 1931. Around 1910, she sent a package to the Cambridge University Library addressed to the librarian, which contained a bundle of suffrage propaganda posters; the reason for her action, however, is unknown. One theory has it that NUWSS member Caroline Mary Ridding, a Sanskrit scholar who was the first woman to be employed at the Cambridge library, may have persuaded Philips to provide the posters for posterity. Alternatively, their delivery could have been at the request of librarian Francis Jenkinson who valued disposable literature such as leaflets, postcards and posters and is known to have gathered a vast collection during the First World War. While collecting such items is now customary for historians, a hundred years ago it was rare, as these items were seen as 'unconsidered trifles'. The bundle was rediscovered in 2016 still covered in its original brown paper wrapping and today, it is one of the largest collections of suffrage posters from the era.

The survival of these posters is very unusual. They would have typically been plastered on walls, fences, or post-boxes, so they would be ripped down soon after being put up, often by people who rejected the cause, property owners, or over time by the weather. They would be printed and distributed to provide information on meetings or events, often ones that were taking place that evening. In addition to seeing posters like these, visitors and residents in Cambridge would also encounter suffrage campaigners on market stalls, handing out literature on the streets such as handbills (small, printed notices distributed by hand), and they could visit a permanent suffrage shop on Bene't Street that sold merchandise to raise money for the cause.

Much like newspapers, posters used attention-grabbing headlines and often had eye-catching pictures, whether cartoons, sketches or photographs, to convey different aspects of the cause. The artists who designed the posters ensured that they would capture the attention of both the public and the press. This came in many forms; for example, it could be an image of a small, slender woman being forcibly arrested by a large, brutish-looking police officer, or a female prisoner getting force-fed. They understood that to win hearts and minds, they often needed to gain the sympathies of the observer.

Posters could be aimed at women in general and intended for distribution nationwide, while some targeted specific groups. For example, some posters were aimed at working-class women, such as those who worked in the textile industry or as seamstresses. They aimed to highlight the injustice of women being denied the right to vote on issues that directly affected that group, and to argue that male voters should not be trusted to vote for what was best for them. The resurfaced collection is an example of posters explicitly targeting women in a particular area – in this case, Cambridge. As a result, many of the subjects are dressed as if they were academics who, despite being educated, were seen by the authorities as criminals or lunatics for protesting for their right to vote.

By the end of the nineteenth century, some women were allowed to study at Cambridge but were not permitted to graduate with full degrees. Although Cambridge was not always progressive in its approach to women's issues, it did establish women's colleges early on, namely

Girton, founded in 1869, and Newnham, which was established two years later. They boasted among their students some of the most active suffrage societies in the country but despite this, Girton College also had at least one anti-suffrage society. When a vote was held in 1897 to allow women to gain full degrees, angry crowds of male students burned effigies of women in protest. The university members voted against the motion, and it was not until 1948 that women were granted the opportunity to graduate from the institution.

Mary Lowndes and the Artist's Suffrage League

Mary Lowndes (1857–1929) was the eldest of eight siblings and the daughter of Richard Lowndes, a first-class cricketer and the vicar of St Mary's Church in Dorset. At the age of 26, she enrolled in the Slade School of Fine Art and two years later, in 1885, she created her first piece of stained glass, a memorial to her grandmother which was installed in her father's church. She went on to be very successful in this field, and much of her work can still be found today in the churches of London and Sussex. Her bold colour choices would be definitive for stained glass during the Arts and Crafts Movement, which began around 1880 in Britain, and celebrated traditional medieval, romantic and folk decoration styles. She would have work exhibited at the Royal Society of British Artists, the Society of Women Artists, Manchester City Art Gallery and the Walker Art Gallery. In 1907, she helped establish the Women's Guild of Arts, which allowed female artists to gather, discuss, debate, and showcase their work. It served as an alternative professional body to the Art Workers Guild, that was established in 1884 and at the time was only open male members.

As a supporter of women's enfranchisement, Lowndes utilised her artistic skills and knowledge to further the cause. She was a member of the London Society for Women's Suffrage and a leading member of the NUWSS, where she served on the executive committee. She would go on to found and lead the Artist's Suffrage League (ASL) in early 1907 to help with the protest commonly known as the Mud

March, for which they produced around eighty banners that were carried by some of the 4,000 people that marched that day.

After the success of the Mud March, members of the ASL would meet at Lowndes' home and studio in Chelsea to create various artworks, including drawings, posters, postcards and banners for use at suffrage events and to be published in papers such as *The Common Cause*. Lowndes also collaborated with other suffrage societies, such as the Women's Writers' Suffrage League, when, along with Dora Meeson Coates and Charlotte Hedley Charlton, she provided drawings to accompany the poems in the 1908 book *Beware! A Warning to Suffragists*. She contributed articles and artwork to the feminist journal *The Englishwoman's Review*, and worked with the WSPU, using their purple, white and green colours, and combining them with bright tones of blue, magenta and orange, which were incredibly impactful when accompanied by bold shapes and simple, designed illustrations.

In 1909, the ASL organised a competition on behalf of the NUWSS, allowing artists to submit their posters. The winner was awarded a prize of £5, with several runners-up receiving £1 each. The aim was to produce posters that were good enough for use in the upcoming elections. One of the winners was Duncan Grant, who created the entry called 'Handicapped!' which is considered one of the decade's most successful suffrage poster designs. Emily Ford was vice-chairman of the organisation and had been a suffrage campaigner since joining the Manchester Society for Women's Suffrage in 1886. She produced one of the group's most famous posters called 'Factory Acts? They Have a Cheek. I've Never Been Asked.' It was a response to several parliamentary acts that shaped the laws surrounding women factory workers and a comment on the fact that women had no say in these laws. The same work was also featured on postcards and in an article in *The Common Cause* magazine.

In the same year, the group produced four posters, six postcards and two Christmas card designs to further their propaganda campaign, and created banners for the Pageant of Women's Trades and Professions, sponsored by the International Suffrage Alliance. Although much of the work was undertaken by Lowndes herself, she also employed the talents of other artists who shared her political views including, Emily Ford, Barbara Forbes, May H. Barker, Clara Billing, Dora Meeson Coates, Violet Garrard, Bertha Newcombe, Charlotte Hedly Charlton and Emily J. Harding. After receiving numerous requests from women to help them with tips on designing their own banners, she published a seven-page pamphlet through the ASL in which she advised on the best dimensions to use, pole size, the use of easily recognisable symbols, and how to choose colours wisely. In the pamphlet, she advises:

> A banner is a thing to float in the wind, to flicker in the breeze, to flirt its colours for your pleasure, to half show and half conceal a device you long to unravel, you do not want to read it, you want to worship it. Choose purple and gold for ambitions, red for courage, green for long-cherished hopes.
>
> Mary Lowndes. *Banners and Banner Making*. The Artist's Suffrage League (1909).

Today, an album of her work can be found in the Women's Library at the London School of Economics, England's foremost library and museum for resources on the women's movement. Mary Lowndes never married and lived with her 'lifelong companion' Barbara Forbes, the secretary of the Artists' Suffrage League, until she died in 1929, leaving Forbes a large sum of money, along with all her artwork and her shares in *The Englishwoman Ltd*.

Cicely Hamilton – The Women Writers Suffrage League and the Actress's Franchise League

Cicely Mary Hammill (1872–1952) was born in London to a Scottish father, Lieutenant-Colonel Denzil Hammill, a decorated officer, and her Irish mother, who mysteriously left the family when Cicely was young, possibly dying soon after. Cicely was educated at St Leonard's boarding school in Malvern and in Bad Homburg, Germany. Soon after leaving school, she began writing and acting in the theatre under the stage name Cicely Hamilton. She also worked as a teaching assistant to make some money, but lost her job after refusing to get a part for her manager's mistress. Throughout her career, she achieved success as a playwright, novelist, journalist, and travel writer, while also being an accomplished actor and a renowned activist.

While she supported the suffrage movement, her main concern was that women were too reliant on men and, as a result, had limited options in life and were usually destined for marriage and motherhood, whether they wanted it or not. She joined the WFL after it split from the WSPU in 1907 and became the editor of its newspaper, *The Vote*. Hamilton was a founding member of two suffrage organisations in 1908, the Women Writers Suffrage League (WWSL) and its sister organisation, the Actress's Franchise League (AFL). She co-wrote the play *How the Vote Was Won* (with Christabel Marshall) in 1908, which was performed by the AFL the following year. It was a fictional account of how women would win the vote in the future and featured an anti-suffragist who has a change of heart when the women in his life decide to strike.

Her most popular suffrage play, written in 1909, was titled *A Pageant of Great Women* and was set in a courtroom to highlight the legal arguments for female suffrage. 'Woman' (played by Hamilton herself) argued the case in favour of women getting the vote, and 'Prejudice' argued against it with the whole thing being played out before the judge, 'Justice'. The play raised awareness for the movement and gave talking points for women who might find themselves debating the subject. In the play, the suffrage argument was won after more than fifty great women of history gave testimony on their contributions to the world. It was performed throughout the country and remained popular with audiences until the start of the First World War.

Hamilton joined the board of the *Englishwoman's Review* in 1909 and was instrumental in helping to found the Women's Tax

Resistance League the same year. Her book, *Marriage as a Trade*, was also published in the same year and was adapted for the stage under *Just to Get Married*, which played to audiences across Britain and New York. The following year, she wrote the lyrics to the song *The March of the Women*, which was composed by Ethel Smyth. The song became the official anthem of the WSPU and was used more widely by members of the suffrage movement at rallies, protests and while in prison.

During the First World War, she worked as an ambulance driver and an administrator in a military hospital in France, then later performed for the troops in France and Belgium from 1917 to 1919. Once the war was over, she returned to England. In 1920, she travelled to Geneva, where she assisted in managing a conference of the Women's International Suffrage Alliance as a press officer. Cicely Hamilton continued to work for women's rights in the 1920s and was not afraid to advocate for what were then controversial subjects such as abortion and contraception. She joined Lady Rhondda's Six-Point Group and was an active member throughout the decade, also serving as a member of the Open-Door Council. She wrote her autobiography, *Life Errant*, in 1935 and died in Chelsea in 1952.

> And now into public life comes trooping the feminine; and
> with the feminine creature come the banners of past times.
>
> Mary Lowndes. *Banners and*
> *Banner Making*. The Artist's
> Suffrage League (1909).

CHAPTER FOUR

Social Class and Identity in the Suffrage Movement

As the suffrage organisations were not generally campaigning for votes for working-class women, relatively few were involved in the early days of the movement. However, soon after the conception of the WSPU it was decided that as women from the lower orders were so numerous in the country, their support was vital. It was also considered that the female vote was necessary for working-class women because it would facilitate the resolution of issues that affected them directly, employment rights in particular. It was argued that female representation in Parliament, even from other social classes, would benefit them more than male parliamentary representation would, and the only way to achieve this was for women to gain the vote on equal terms as men.

Sylvia Pankhurst, a staunch advocate for working-class women, often spoke of the lack of interest in them from her mother and sister Christabel, claiming they favoured people from their own, middle class, social strata. Christabel denied this and showed it to be untrue when she rejected an alliance with the Daily Herald League, which practised militant industrialism. She claimed that theirs was a class struggle whereas the WSPU welcomed members from all walks of life, as long as they were women. This is probably a more accurate view of the organisation, and it led to the unusual scenario of working-class women, such as Annie Kenney, having authority over middle and upper-class women.

Annie Kenney – The Working-Class Poster Girl

Annie Kenney (1879–1953) was one of twelve children born to parents who worked in the cotton mills of Oldham, Greater Manchester. From the age of 10 she worked part-time at Henry Atherton and Son's textile mill, working from 6 am until 12.30 pm; like many in the industry, she lost a finger in an accident involving the machinery. After her shift, she would head to school until 5 pm, until at 13 years old she left her education behind and began working full-time. She stated in her autobiography, *Memories of a Militant* (1924), that she left school with little knowledge, having a poor grasp of subjects such as writing, mathematics and geography, but was a keen reader of poetry. Her mother, Ann, instilled in her a love of learning. Regular debates and discussions between the Kenney family and their friends taught Annie that statements without proof should not be accepted blindly. These family learning sessions would stand her in good stead in the future as she became a renowned public speaker for the WSPU, as well as an excellent organiser and an enthusiastic worker. It also made her the ideal working-class poster girl for the movement as she combined the typical image of the downtrodden, vulnerable factory girl who needed uplifting, with that of an exceptional woman of her station, who was articulate, intelligent, and highly motivated for the cause.

While in the mill, she became a member of the ILP. She utilised her organisational skills to become a trade union official, representing 69,000 female cotton mill workers. During an ILP meeting in 1905, the then 26-year-old, and her 18-year-old sister Jessie, heard Christabel Pankhurst and Teresa Billington-Greig speak, and she was hooked; before this, she had never even heard of the concept of votes for women. After the meeting, she walked with Christabel and was invited to the Pankhurst house the following Saturday. Soon after, she handed out copies of a handbill written by Christabel and gave her first public speech to a crowd off Market Square in Manchester, a task that had terrified her at first. She wrote of the early days in the WSPU:

> The changed life into which most of us entered was a revolution in itself. No home life, no one to say what we should do or what we should not do, no family ties, we were free and alone in a great brilliant city, scores of young women scarcely out of their teens met together in a revolutionary movement, outlaws or breakers of laws, independent of everything and everybody, fearless and self-confident.
>
> Annie Kenney. *Memories of a Militant*. Edward Arnold and Co (1924).

From there, Kenney would speak regularly in working-class areas of Lancashire to garner support and recruit new members for the WSPU. She would dress in traditional working attire such as clogs and a shawl, often standing on the streets or at factory gates to talk to women as they left work. She also continued to attend ILP meetings, delivering speeches to appeal to other politically active working-class women, asserting that winning the vote was imperative and that the militant strategy was the most effective way to achieve it.

As a result of the limited number of working-class women involved in the movement, Kenney was urged to leave her job and help establish and run the Canning Town branch of the WSPU in the East End of London. On 19 February 1906, Emmeline Pankhurst, Dora Montefiore and Annie Kenney spoke to hundreds of women who had gathered in Parliament Square at the state opening of Parliament to demonstrate for the cause of women's suffrage. Many upper-class women attended, but disguised themselves in the clothing of their maids as they did not want to be recognised, showing that many still worried about the stigma of association with the militant cause at this time. However, this was not the case for the leading members of the WSPU.

A group of suffragettes, including Emmeline and Christabel Pankhurst, travelled to Northampton on 14 June 1906, to heckle the future Prime Minister and then Chancellor of the Exchequer, Herbert H. Asquith. As they shouted, things got heated, and both men and women in the crowd attacked them. Teresa Billington-Greig had arrived in a long, flowing gown, making her appear like a duchess. She pulled out a whip that she had concealed in her dress and started lashing at the heads and shoulders of nearby men before she was tackled by three of them and forced down some steps, causing her dress to rip. Undeterred, she urged her fellow protesters to attack the Chancellor when he left the meeting; as he did, Kenney – dressed like a grieving widow – tried to do just that but was grabbed by a policeman before she could get to him.

Five days later, eight women, including Kenney and Billington-Greig, went to the Chancellor's house but he refused to see them and slipped away unnoticed. Two days after that, on 21 June, nearly 200 women were at his house, causing a 'tremendous commotion'. Once again, he refused to see them, and when she pressed the issue Kenney was arrested, which was met with cheers by some of Asquith's servants, much to the dismay of the onlooking suffragettes. She would serve six weeks in Holloway with fellow Canning Town WSPU members, Adelaide Knight and the 64-year-old Jane Sbarborough.

In an edition of the *Portsmouth Evening News* on 3 September 1906, Kenney was described as speaking, 'The King's English perfectly with a delightful roll, the effect of which is heightened by her vivacity and her intense earnestness.' Poet Phoebe Hesketh wrote in her biography of her aunt Edith Rigby, *My Aunt Edith* (1966), that Kenney's speaking style was 'Full of punch and pith' with a 'salty sense of humour'. For example, she once stated sarcastically that if they did not win the vote for women, 'we'll see lads of 21 making laws for their own mothers!' She frequently attended meetings and photo opportunities wearing her mill clothes, clogs, and a shawl covering her head to attract more interest from her social class. The pictures of her dressed this way were made into postcards and used in shop window displays as part of the WSPU's propaganda campaign. On 21 March 1907, the *London Daily News* described one such photo of her as being 'a romantic and defiant figure in the shawl of a millhand'.

While playing the part of a working-class hero was sometimes appropriate, at other times it was considered that the best way to impress an audience was to dress more like a lady of means. This lack of consistency made some sceptical of the image she portrayed, believing it to be unauthentic. An article in the *Leeds Mercury* on 21 May 1906, stated:

> Her brand-new woollen shawl and her coquettish clogs bore about as much resemblance to the everyday articles of the Lancashire streets as a field marshal's uniform bears to the working clothes of the militiaman after a month's training.

While it is true that these photos were displayed for the spectacle, they still represented her background, so they at least had an air of authenticity. That said, she was aware that class was being used as a tool through her. When it came to the poorest women, she later expressed doubt as to her usefulness to them, stating:

> How I had the courage and audacity to talk votes for women to those thin, sallow, pinched, pain-stricken, poverty-lined faces I do not know … Poor oppressed, unawakened East-Enders – every reformer using them for his own ends, and we were doing just the same!
>
> Annie Kenney. *Memories of a Militant.*
> Edward Arnold and Co (1924).

Much was made of the juxtaposition between Kenney and Christabel. Teresa Billington-Greig described them in an article from the *Aberdeen People's Journal* in March 1907, stating:

One of them was a mill girl who had a bitter experience of the restrictions to which working women are subjected. The other was a daughter of a lawyer, herself studying to be a lawyer. Together, they represented the two forces that are the life of this new women's agitation: the need of women, as typified by Annie Kenney, and the rebellion of educated women against restrictions, represented by Christabel Pankhurst.

A lot of emphasis was clearly put on Kenney's working-class status by the WSPU, which initially helped with early recruitment and acquired attention from the press. It can be argued that over time, she would connect more with middle-class suffragettes than those of her own social class and as the movement focused on attracting more members from wealthier backgrounds, the focus on Kenney shifted and she began to be celebrated and appreciated for her commitment and contributions to the cause, irrespective of her social class. What's more, her ability to attract members from the middle classes proved equal to her ability to bring in working-class women. In a March 1908 edition of *Votes for Women*, she pointed out that before attending the upcoming Women's Parliament, working-class women had to 'Bake the bread, to do the washing, and prepare for their husbands and families', she went on to urge 'the women of social standing present to fight for the cause themselves, and to go to prison if necessary and not to let the working-women do all the fighting'.

Her brother Rowland was a manual labourer in his younger years but later became a journalist, editor of the *Daily Herald*, and a publisher of *Vanity Fair*. He was also a member of the ILP and was critical of working-class women who joined the suffrage movement, believing them to be manipulated. He wrote an article titled 'The Militant Movement in Ruins', published in *The English Review* in 1912. In it, he stated:

Their minds were easily played upon by the displayed smartness and wealth of their leaders … they liked to be among women who were obviously clever, well-bred and in easy circumstances; it flattered their vanity and was a welcome change in life, which, God knows, they needed.

While it's true that working-class women were used strategically at times, arguing that they were manipulated into acting for the cause is patronising at best. Many, including Kenney, often acted on their own initiative, and those who suffered for the cause – for example by being attacked or getting arrested – did so of their own accord and often at significant cost to themselves.

While Annie Kenney loved the people she worked with and saw many women from a higher social status as her kin, she never lost sight of her roots. On 19 August 1913, she took a trip to France along with her sister Jessie, Mary Richardson and Ida Wylie. She stayed with Christabel Pankhurst, Oliver Belmont and his wife Alva, an American multimillionaires and suffrage activist. Despite years of working with, and being in charge of, many people of a higher class than her, she found it difficult to relax in this situation. Having to put on airs and graces, to dress up and even to wear white gloves every day was too much for her, so after a week or so she left to stay at the La Guimorais in Brittany. She described it as closer to her 'gypsy heart' and said that her time there was filled with laughter.

During the First World War, she toured the country with Emmeline Pankhurst, Flora Drummond and Grace Roe before going to France and the USA, recruiting and lecturing on women's war work. She married James Taylor in 1918 and bore him a son, Warwick Kenney Taylor. The family settled in Letchworth, where she lived until she died in 1953, at the age of 73.

Minnie Baldock – Founding Member of the Canning Town WSPU

Lucy 'Minnie' Baldock (1864–1954) was one of Annie Kenney's closest friends and had worked in a shirt factory in conditions described as a 'sweatshop', characterised by poor sanitation, low health and safety standards, long hours and starvation wages. In 1892, she joined the Independent Labour Party and campaigned for improved pay and working conditions for women, even jointly chairing a meeting with Keir Hardie to protest the low wages paid to women. In 1903, she was tasked, along with fellow suffragette Charlotte Despard, with distributing the local unemployment fund used to alleviate extreme poverty in East London.

She was an early devotee of the WSPU and, along with Kenney, one of the few working-class members of the organisation to rise beyond the rank and file. On 21 December 1905, Kenney planned to ask the Prime Minister Sir Henry Campbell-Bannerman when he spoke at a pre-election meeting of the Liberals at the Royal Albert Hall if his party would introduce votes for women. Kenney sent him a letter stating that she wanted the answer in writing or that she would ask him in person at the event; Campbell-Bannerman ignored the correspondence, so she had Keir Hardie purchase her tickets. She then disguised herself as a wealthy lady, complete with a fur coat and a veil, and was closely followed by Baldock, who pretended to be her maid.

After being led to a private box, they hung a banner over the edge that read, 'Votes for Women', and shouted, 'Will the Liberal Government give women the vote?' At the same time, Teresa Billington-Greig, who had also gained access, unfurled a banner that read, 'Will the Liberal Government give justice to working women?' There was uproar but the organist was instructed to play loudly to drown out the noise and the politicians ignored the questions. The ladies were removed from the building, though none of them were arrested on this occasion. The next day, Kenney, Billington-Greig and Baldock went to the Prime Minister's house to ask him again. This time he told them he would address the issue 'soon', which was seen as a minor victory for the women. Dora Montefiore, who was at the Royal Albert Hall but did not participate in the disturbance, sent a postcard to Minnie Baldock congratulating her and the others on their 'noble stand'. Montefiore had devised the tactic of asking Liberal politicians directly if they would give women the vote should they be elected and was pleased to see the idea adopted by other members of the WSPU.

Kenney and Baldock were seen as the ideal women to convey the Suffragettes' message to the poverty-stricken East End of London so in 1906 they formed the Canning Town WSPU, the first branch to be established in the capital. Many of the Canning Town suffragettes were sympathetic to Teresa Billington-Greig's point of view when, in 1907, she formed the breakaway organisation, the Women's Freedom League. Many were supporters of the ILP and believed in the democratic process, which led to many working-class women who did not join the WFL drifting away from the movement altogether. By 3 December 1907, only fifteen attended a meeting and only threepence ha'penny was collected, the smallest WSPU collection on record. Entries in the Canning Town branch of the WSPU for the minutes book end on 10 December, which is the last surviving information on the ground-breaking branch.

Baldock remained with the WSPU and continued to speak at various events and would serve prison time for her beliefs. The first time she was arrested was in 1906, when she was charged with disorderly conduct for shouting 'votes for women' through a megaphone during the opening of Parliament. In February 1908, she was arrested again, this time alongside Annie Kenney, Emmeline Pankhurst and seven other women for resisting and obstructing the police while protesting the lack of political status afforded to suffragettes while incarcerated. They were all sentenced to a month in prison, and while she was serving her time, her fellow suffragettes helped her husband care for their two children, sending them toys and prompting her younger son, Jack, to write a thank-you letter in which he stated that he was proud of his mother.

In 1910, Baldock was diagnosed with cancer and underwent surgery performed by Louise Aldrich-Blake, one of Britain's first female surgeons. After her recovery, she broke ties with the increasingly militant WSPU, although she remained a member of the Church League for Women's Suffrage. In the 1911 census her name was absent, suggesting she was one of the many suffrage campaigners who boycotted it. Even though she had cut ties with the suffragettes, in 1928 she participated in the funeral of Emmeline Pankhurst and two years later, she attended the unveiling of a statue dedicated to the founder of the WSPU. She helped Edith How-Martyn and the Suffragette Fellowship document the movement's history, and died at the age of 90 in 1954.

Clara Codd – Downward Social Mobility

Clara Codd (1876–1971) was a middle-class woman from Devon and the eldest of ten girls, all of whom were educated at home by a series of governesses. With her father's death in 1899, the family moved to Geneva because of financial constraints. She had to work to help out so she took on a number of jobs, including working as a translator, a costume model, travelling around France and Switzerland as a concert pianist and violinist – all before finding work as a governess. She later wrote of her interactions in Switzerland in her autobiography *So Rich a Life* (1951), 'I came into contact with all sorts and conditions of men and learned to be free and a friend of all that lives, instead of the proper, little caste-ridden Victorian that I was in the beginning.'

After hearing Annie Kenney speak in 1907, she resigned from her position as a governess and joined the WSPU. She helped organise a visit to the south-east of England for Kenney and Christabel Pankhurst, and a year later she was made secretary of the WSPU branch in Bath. Kenney asked a wealthy member to help her with ten shillings a week to cover her expenses and put Codd up in her own room, with the two sharing a large double bed. She stated in her autobiography, 'Occasionally I woke to find Annie trying to throttle me! In her dreams, she was still fighting battles.'

Both Codd and Kenney were attacked in one incident in Bath, leaving them needing a police escort to escape the baying crowd. Sometimes, when chalking messages on pavements, she would be attacked by police or members of the public; in the case of the latter, it would be local women rather than men who shrieked at her and chased her away. Kenney often sent Codd and other members to start speeches, drawing anti-suffragette crowds. However, these decoys allowed Kenney's own speech, held nearby, to incur less interruption. In one incident, the crowd realised they had been duped and surrounded Codd and her friend. This time, a nearby policeman refused to help with a 'frightening, sardonic smile', and someone tried to stab her with a blunt instrument, causing her to run. As she did so, the crowd threw mud and offal at her before she was helped onto a tram by a 'kind man'.

She was one of thirty-seven people arrested during the Rush on Parliament on 13 October 1908 and was sentenced to a month in prison. She spent some of her time in solitary confinement and, as a vegetarian, found her options for food limited. Towards the end of 1908, she was offered a paid role with the WSPU but declined. The following year she drifted away from the suffragettes, appearing to have played no further part in the movement. Clara Codd died in Berkshire in 1971.

The Diaries of Emily and Mary Blathwayt

Mary Blathwayt (1879–1961) was the eldest of the two children of upper-middle-class parents, Colonel Linley Blathwayt (1839–1919) and his wife Emily (1852–1940). Until her mid-twenties, Mary led a relatively quiet life, though she kept herself busy in various ways. She was a member of the Avon Vale Musical Society and, along with her mother, spent much of her time teaching music to children in a nearby village. She actively participated in local charitable events and enjoyed gardening and caring for her chickens. Mary and her mother were avid diary writers, and from these documents, we have learned a great deal about the activities of the WSPU in the area and the women who participated in them. They joined the WSPU around 1906 after meeting Annie Kenney and agreed to help her organise in Southwest England, along with Clara Codd and two others, Elsie Howey and Mary Philips.

Linley Blathwayt had retired from the army in 1882 and purchased Eagle House, a mansion on the outskirts of Bath, complete with four acres of land. He supported the suffrage endeavours of his wife and daughter, and soon after they joined the cause Eagle House became a haven for visiting suffragettes. A summerhouse was built which he called 'Suffragettes Rest', where members of the WSPU and other organisations could rest, practice speeches, write letters and as a place they could stay when working in the area. Linley was a keen photographer and would take pictures of the visiting ladies, who would then sign the photographs and sell them to raise funds for their suffrage organisation.

Annie Kenney frequently stayed with the Blathwayts and was treated as a member of the family, despite the gap in social status. On one occasion, Linley taught her to drive, and on another, Mary taught her to swim, also giving her regular French lessons. Although they were well-respected members of the WSPU and friends with Kenney and many other suffragettes, Emily and Mary primarily engaged in non-militant activism; in 1907 Mary also became a member of the NUWSS.

In the following year, she even met Millicent Garrett Fawcett through her friend, Lilias Ashworth Hallett, who was also a member of both organisations, and expressed surprise that Fawcett looked so young considering she had worked towards women's suffrage for around forty years. She spent much of 1908 and 1909 working closely with Kenney, speaking at open-air meetings, writing their message in chalk on pavements, and selling pamphlets to help spread the word about the fight for women's suffrage. In the 11 February 1909 edition of *Votes for Women*, Emmeline Pethick-Lawrence praised the Blathwayt family while calling for more volunteers from the middle and upper classes to help the cause:

> I say to you young women who have private means or whose parents are able and willing to support you while they give you freedom to choose your vocation. Come

and dedicate one year of your life to sharing the message of deliverance with thousands of your sisters. Complete a short training course under the guidance of one of our senior officers or at our headquarters in London, and then become one of our honorary staff organisers. Miss Annie Kenney, in the West of England, has two such honorary organisers. Miss Blathwayt is the only daughter of Colonel Lindley Blathwayt, of Bath. Yet her parents have set her free with their fullest approbation and sympathy, and with a generous allowance, to devote her whole time to the work.

There are hints in Mary Blathwayt's diary that she and Christabel Pankhurst had a romantic relationship before Christabel began an affair with Annie Kenney. Teresa Billington-Greig believed that Kenney was 'emotionally possessed' by Christabel, but Mary saw it the other way around, stating that Kenney had a 'wonderful influence over people'. It is unclear how many lesbian relationships Kenney had, if any, as the subject was seldom discussed or even recognised in the early twentieth century. Still, some historians believe it likely that some of her friendships, as well as some of Christabel's, were romantic in nature, as alluded to in Mary's diaries. After she shared a bed with Kenney in 1908 she appeared to be jealous in an entry stating, 'Miss Browne is sleeping in Annie's room now'. She seems to suggest that Kenney had slept with at least ten WSPU members at Eagle House, including Christabel and Clara Codd, who confirmed in her autobiography *So Rich a Life* that she slept with Kenney on 7 September 1910.

Another school of thought is that Mary was very literal, and her words should not be seen in the context of lesbianism. Instead, it is argued that Kenney's relationships were close friendships, and that when Mary said 'sleeping together', no sexual intimacy was implied. Clara Codd would often give her reason for sleeping with Kenney, as it simply being a way to save money (though this would not apply at Eagle House), and Kenney's adoration for Christabel could be interpreted as a form of 'sisterly' love. This is supported by the fact that when she was released from prison in 1905, she stayed with the Pankhurst family for a while, and Emmeline promised her that she would always have a home with them.

From April 1909, when suffragettes and suffragists arrived at Eagle House, they would plant a tree as a peaceful protest to the force-feeding of suffragettes while in prison. The garden became known as *Annie's Arboretum* in honour of Annie Kenney, who may have suggested the idea. Although Mary only participated in non-militant activities, the work was not always safe for her and her colleagues. On 8 June 1909, she wrote in her diary of an experience she and Elsie Howey, the middle-class daughter of a parish rector, suffered while at a public meeting in Bristol. They were speaking from the back of a lorry when the crowd began throwing things. They drove away with the two ladies still in the back of the lorry and were pelted with potatoes, stones, turf and dust. Howey was hit and had a cut lip and Mary was hit in the ear. The incident could have been worse as 'someone threw a big stone as big as a baby's head; it fell onto the lorry'.

Emily Blathwayt resigned from the WSPU in September 1909 after the Prime Minister was assaulted by Vera Wentworth, Elsie Howey and Jessie Kenney. Her husband wrote letters of complaint to the women involved and banned Howey and Wentworth from Eagle House. Wentworth responded with an understanding of their reaction but told him, 'If Mr Asquith will not receive deputation, they will pummel him again.' She expressed unhappiness in her diary in November 1912 that her daughter was spending all day in Bath working on the suffrage campaign, writing, 'Supporters are fast leaving the WSPU, especially those old in years, but people like Miss Lamb do not at all like Mrs Pankhurst's present policy.'

As the militancy of the WSPU increased, Mary's support for the organisation also wavered, perhaps due to pressure from her parents. When an arson attack in June 1913 destroyed a nearby house, she resigned from the WSPU, though she remained a member of the

NUWSS as her mother had done. Emily wrote in her diary soon after, 'I am glad to say Mary is writing to resign membership with the WSPU. Now they have begun burning houses in the neighbourhood, I feel more than ever ashamed to be connected with them.'

Both women spent the rest of their lives at Eagle House, with Emily passing away in 1940, at approximately 88 years old, and Mary in 1961, at 82 years old. After Mary's death, Eagle House was sold, and 'Suffragettes Rest' was bulldozed to make way for a housing estate. However, new trees have since been planted, along with replacements for the memorials that were destroyed in the process. The diaries of Emily and Mary Blathwayt are kept at the Gloucestershire Archives and along with the numerous photographs taken by Linley, provide us with a unique and personal insight into the women behind the movement. They show that they came from diverse backgrounds with differing opinions on how the cause should be fought but ultimately were united behind the common goal of female suffrage.

Vera Holme – The Cross-Dressing Suffragette

Vera Holme (1881–1969), commonly known as 'Jack' or 'Jacko', was the daughter of a middle-class timber merchant from Lancashire. When she was a teenager, her parents split up and although her father occasionally gave her an allowance as she grew older, it did not cover her living expenses. Consequently, she found work as an artist's model, a singer and an actor. In 1903, she signed a contract to become a male impersonator on stage, earning her a substantial sum for the time. She lived on the road for several years working with travelling theatrical companies, and it is thought that her nickname 'Jack' was derived from a male character she developed during this period. In contrast, from 1906 to 1909, she performed with the women's chorus in the D'Oyly Carte Opera Company's Gilbert and Sullivan London Repertory Seasons at the Savoy Theatre, where she wore extravagant gowns that appealed to the wealthy audiences.

She helped form the Actress' Franchise League in 1908 and with them, would sing outside Holloway Prison in support of the suffragettes incarcerated there. Sometime in the same year, she joined the WSPU, and soon after, she began working with Annie Kenney and Clara Codd, frequently visiting Eagle House. Emily Blathwayt stated in her diary that Holme is a 'splendid woman who is interested in all of Linley's subjects; she took up Mary's violin and was very clever with it. She has a beautiful voice, and we sang after washing up.' However, not everyone admired her, and Sylvia Pankhurst once described her as 'a noisy, explosive young person, frequently rebuked by her elders for lack of dignity'. When the suffragettes protested at Hyde Park in 1909, she dressed as a mounted officer complete with horse. In the same year, at the Pageant of Great Women, a play frequently performed by members of the AFL, she dressed as Hannah Snell, who in 1747 had disguised herself as a man to join the British military.

Her most famous protest with the WSPU was organised by Annie Kenney and was carried out in conjunction with Minnie Baldock and Elsie Howey. Augustine Birrell was a Liberal Member of Parliament and Secretary of State for Ireland. He was due to make a speech at Colston Hall in Bristol on 1 May 1909, and though the venue would not allow women to attend, this did not stop the WSPU from infiltrating. The events were described in a series of letters to Kenney from Constance Lytton, sent in the following weeks, which stated that Howey and Holme attended a concert at Colston Hall the night before. When it finished, they hid in the cloakroom and when the building reopened the next day, they headed to the main hall and hid behind a large organ. Armed with megaphones, they shouted slogans such as 'votes for women' when Birrell was making his speech, and when he spoke about liberty one of them shouted, 'Why don't you give women liberty?' The crowd was in uproar, cheering, booing and mostly laughing as the stewards repeatedly tried to get the ladies out of the organ while they continued to shout. Eventually, they were caught and removed from the venue, though neither of them was arrested on this occasion.

That summer, Holme became the official chauffeur for the leaders of the WSPU, for which she wore a uniform made out of the suffragette colours along with a peaked cap. Her predecessor was Aileen Preston, the first woman to pass the Automobile Association Certificate in Driving successfully. In 1911 Holme would be described in the trade journal *The Chauffeur* as an excellent driver and a skilled mechanic.

Although there is some ambiguity over the sexuality of Annie Kenney, Clara Codd and others, the same cannot be said for Holme, who was certainly lesbian. In 1910 she befriended fellow WSPU member Evelina Haverfield, the daughter of William Scarlett, the third Baron Abinger. The two, along with scientist Alice Laura Embleton, known as Alick, and her partner Celia Wray, would get together in what is believed to have been a secret lesbian society, of which the membership was restricted to suffragettes. Haverfield had two sons with her first husband, Henry Tunstall Haverfield, and remarried in 1899 to John Balguy, four years after Henry's death, although she refused to take her new husband's name. She wrote in her diary on her wedding day, 'I married Major Balguy with no intention of changing my name or mode of life in any way. He is an old friend of my darling Jack.' After around ten years, the two separated but never divorced.

Haverfield was arrested for the cause several times over the years, including at a demonstration in 1910 when she hit a police officer in the mouth. The statement made on her charge sheet asserted that she said, 'It was not hard enough. Next time I will bring a revolver.' Vera Holme herself was arrested at least three times and went to prison at least once, when she served five days for obstructing the police after throwing stones on 22 November 1911. Holme and Haverfield lived together in Devon from 1911. Holme changed her will a year later, leaving everything to Haverfield, including a bed with 'E.H. & V.H.' carved onto its sides. From around this time, she used Jack as her identification more often than not, and the pictures that remain of her suggest she usually wore men's clothes and adopted masculine habits, as did Evelina Haverfield. In today's language, she may be considered to have been transgender or gender fluid, but in her lifetime, these terms were not around, so how she identified is less clear.

During the war, Holme joined the Women's Volunteer Reserve, founded by Haverfield. She later followed her partner to the Scottish Women's Hospitals for Foreign Service (SWH), where she drove horse-drawn and motorised ambulances. In 1915, they went to Serbia and refused to leave when it became dangerous, leading to both getting captured and held as prisoners of war, though they were released a year later. After serving as an ambulance driver in Romania and Russia, Holme returned to Britain and lectured around the country to raise money for the SWH. Holme and Haverfield remained partners, although Holme spent some time at an artist's colony, where she had an affair with the Scottish painter Dorothy Johnstone. Holme and Haverfield later moved to Serbia, where they opened and renovated orphanages; Haverfield died in 1920, leaving Holmes £50 a year for life, despite protests from her estranged husband.

By 1923, Holme was living in Scotland and was involved in what was probably a polyamorous relationship with Margaret Greenlees and Margaret Ker until Ker left the relationship in 1939 and Greenlees died in 1952. Vera Holme died in a Glasgow nursing home on 1 January 1969, aged 88, leaving us with her letters, diaries and photographs that give an insight into the terminologies and codes used by lesbians in Britain in the early twentieth century.

Lady Constance Lytton – AKA the Seamstress Jane Warton

Lady Constance Georgina Bulwer-Lytton (1869–1923), commonly known as Lady Constance Lytton, was the third of seven children of the 1st Earl of Lytton, Robert Bulwer-Lytton, and Edith Villiers. Among her siblings were her brothers Victor, a member of the House of Lords and Neville, a decorated military officer and Olympian. One of her sisters, Edith, married Gerald Balfour, the brother of the future Prime Minister Arthur Balfour, and another, Elizabeth, was a fellow suffragette.

Up to the age of 11 she was educated by a series of governesses and lived in India, where her father was the governor-general. The rest of her youth was spent in England surrounded by some of the biggest names in art, literature and politics. However, Lytton's aristocratic life held little attraction for her, and she later stated that she had a lonely childhood. She fell in love with John Ponsonby, a low-ranking officer in the British armed forces, but in 1892 her mother barred her from marrying him due to the class divide between them. Believing her mother might change her mind she refused to marry anybody else, but this did not materialise and she remained unwed for the rest of her life.

She met Emmeline Pethick-Lawrence in September 1908, and in a letter to her friend Adela Smith, she expressed her sympathy with the cause but was critical of some of the WSPU's methods. Prison reform was a passion of hers and after meeting Mrs Pethick-Lawrence again, along with Annie Kenney, she came to realise that the suffragettes suffered the abuses of incarceration first-hand, so she decided to work with them, stating in a letter to her mother on 14 October 1908:

> I went to the Suffragette Office to see Mrs Lawrence and to congratulate her on the meeting of the day before, inquire the latest news, and finally say: 'You know my reservations as to some of your methods, but my sympathies are much more with you than with any of your opponents … I want to be of use if I can. Is there anything I can possibly do to help you?' A good deal of talk ensued. She said, 'Yes,' I could help them. Could I see to it that Herbert Gladstone was asked to treat the Suffragettes as political offenders, which they are, and not as common criminals, which they are not?

Once again Lytton's family disapproved of the company she kept with those of a lower social station than her, but to her, Kenney and the others were her new extended family. In her autobiography *Prisons and Prisoners: Some Personal Experiences* (1914), Lytton described Kenney as a 'woman of great character, courage, and ability', and acknowledged that outside the WSPU, she was Kenney's social superior but her subordinate within it. She saw Kenney and her sibling Jessie as her sisters and signed letters that she wrote to them, 'Sister Conny'.

Even Lytton's mother Edith, who deplored militant suffrage, came to love Annie Kenney and they formed a lasting friendship that endured beyond Constance's death. The fact that a duchess could form a close friendship with a working-class girl from Greater Manchester, with no political ties in common, shows that Kenney could bond with anyone, regardless of their beliefs, generation or social status. This demonstrates why she was so important to recruitment within the movement, and how little social class affected networking for the suffragettes, even if it was with someone who disagreed with their methods.

In January 1909 Lady Constance Lytton became a member of the WSPU, and the following month she participated in a demonstration at the House of Commons, resulting in a one-month stay in Holloway Prison. While there, she was kept in the hospital wing due to her having a weak heart. This preferential treatment infuriated her, so in a bid to be treated the same as any other suffragette she began to self-harm. She aimed to scratch 'Votes for Women' into her skin with a needle and hatpin, with the first letter starting at her heart and the last intended to finish on her face. When she scratched the 'V', she went too deep and doctors had to treat her, though her protest did work as she was soon moved into the general population.

When it was realised that she was the daughter of a lord, authorities, aware of her health problems, feared that if she died in prison she would become a martyr to the cause, so she was released immediately. By October of the same year, she had started to see some merit in militant action. In her autobiography, she wrote:

On Friday, 8th October 1909, Christabel Pankhurst and I were on our way to Newcastle. I had made up my mind that

I was going to throw a stone. We went to the Haymarket
where the car with Mr Lloyd George would probably pass.
As the motor appeared I stepped out into the road, stood
straight in front of the car, shouted out, 'How can you, who
say you back the women's cause, stay on in a government
which refuses them the vote, and is persecuting them for
asking it,' and threw a stone at the car. I aimed low to
avoid injuring the chauffeur or passengers.

Constance Lytton. *Prisons and
Prisoners: Some Personal Experiences.*
William Heinemann (1914).

The stone was wrapped in paper which had written on it, 'To Lloyd
George – Rebellion against tyranny is obedience to God – Deeds, not
words,' which alluded to the motto 'Rebellion to tyrants is obedience
to God', used by Thomas Jefferson for his personal seal and probably
first written by Benjamin Franklin as a suggestion for the official seal
for the USA.

Lytton took part in a demonstration in January 1910 and marched
to the house of the governor of Walton Prison in Liverpool to protest
the treatment of WSPU members who were being force-fed in his
establishment. Anticipating her ensuing arrest and not wanting to
receive preferential treatment, she dressed in working-class clothes
and told the authorities that she was a seamstress named Jane Warton.
Her plan worked, and after going on a hunger strike she was force-fed
eight times; when her true identity was discovered, she was, true to
form, released immediately. She wrote in her autobiography, which
originally named Jane Warton as a co-author:

I joined the WSPU again, filling up the membership card
as Miss Jane Warton. The choice of a name had been easy.
When I came out of Holloway Prison, a distant relative,
by name Mr F. Warburton, wrote me an appreciative
letter, thanking me for having been a prisoner in this

A sketch of a women's suffrage meeting held at St James's Hall, London in 1884. The event was chaired by Elizabeth Garrett Anderson, and speakers such as Lydia Becker called for the inclusion of women's suffrage in the Reform Bill that had recently been put forward by William Gladstone. (People's History Museum. Public domain, via Wikimedia Commons)

A picture of the Mud March in 1907 from the *Illustrated London News*. At the head of the procession are Lady Frances Balfour, Lady Jane Maria Strachey and Milicent Garrett Fawcett, all leading members of the NUWSS. (Credited as 'Topical and Sport and General Illustrations.' Public domain, via Wikimedia Commons)

Left: Published in *Punch Magazine* in January 1906, this illustration by Bernard Partridge depicts a constitutional suffragist berating a member of the WSPU for her militant actions. (John Bernard Partridge. Public domain, via Wikimedia Commons)

Below: Suffragettes selling their newspaper *Votes for Women* in Fleet Street in 1908. (LSE Library. No restrictions, via Wikimedia Commons)

Above: The Putney and Fulham WSPU shop and office in London, photographed by Christina Broom in 1910. (Christina Broom (died 1939). Public domain, via Wikimedia Commons)

Right: An anti-suffrage postcard depicting a man exhausted from doing housework. (LSE Library. No restrictions, via Wikimedia Commons)

Above: Flora Drummond (centre) and the welcome home party, all wearing tartan sashes, for Scottish suffragette Mary Phillips upon her release from prison (*c*.1908). (LSE Library. No restrictions, via Wikimedia Commons)

Left: A suffrage poster from the Cambridge University Library collection rediscovered in 2016. The depiction alludes to the fact that in terms of voting, an educated woman was treated the same as a convict and a person institutionalized with a mental illness. (Emily Jane Harding Andrews (1850 – 1940); restored by Adam Cuerden. Public domain, via Wikimedia Commons)

Above left: *Handicapped* by Duncan Grant. This poster won the competition held by the Artists Suffrage League in 1909 and is considered one of the most successful propaganda posters of its day. (LSE Library. No restrictions, via Wikimedia Commons)

Above right: This poster was designed by Emily Ford, vice-chairman of the Artists' Suffrage League in 1908. It intended to highlight the hypocrisy of passing Parliamentary acts that directly affect women without them having any say on what goes into those acts. (Emily Ford. Public domain, via Wikimedia Commons)

Right: Annie Kenney dressed in the traditional attire of a mill worker *c.*1907. (LSE Library. No restrictions, via Wikimedia Commons)

Annie Kenney (left) and Christabel Pankhurst (*c.*1908) holding a banner with the famous WSPU slogan, *Votes for Women*. (hastingspress.co.uk. Public domain, via Wikimedia Commons)

Mary Blathwayt (left) planting a tree at *Annie's Arboretum* along with Vera Holme (left centre), Jessie Kenney (right centre) and Annie Kenney (right). The picture was taken by Mary's father Colonel Linley Blathwayt at Eagle House in 1909. (Linley Blathwayt (died 1919). Public domain, via Wikimedia Commons)

Suffragette chauffeur Vera 'Jack' Holme, taken some time after the summer of 1909. (LSE Library. No restrictions, via Wikimedia Commons)

Princess Sophia Duleep Singh selling copies of the *Suffragette* newspaper outside Hampton Court in 1913. (Museum of London. Public domain, via Wikimedia Commons)

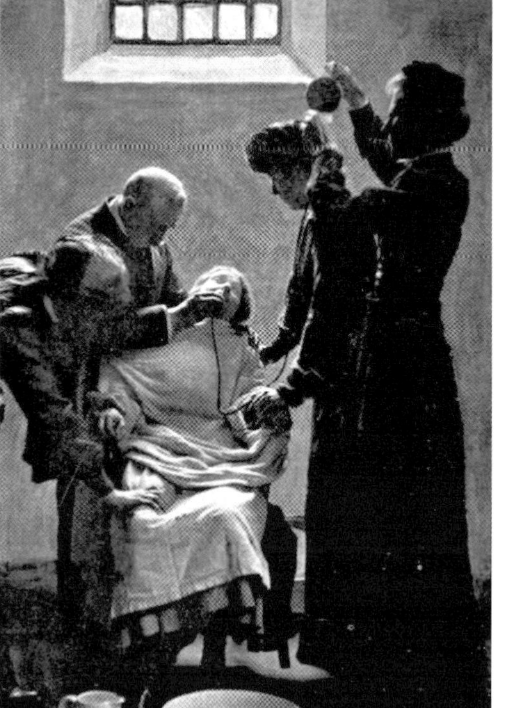

Above: A hunger strike medal awarded to Grace Roe by the WSPU in 1914. (LSE Library. No restrictions, via Wikimedia Commons)

Left: An unknown hunger striking suffragette being force-fed with a nasal tube (*c.*1911). (Unknown author. Public domain, via Wikimedia Commons)

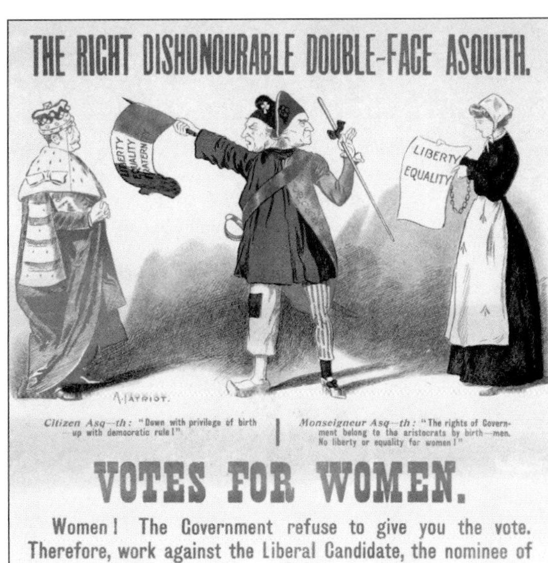

Above: A photograph taken at the gates of Holloway Prison on the 22 August 1908. Mary Leigh and Edith New have just been released and are holding up two inedible loaves of bread that they had snuck out of the prison. (LSE Library. No restrictions, via Wikimedia Commons)

Right: A suffragette poster from 1910 portraying the Prime Minister Herbert H. Asquith and accusing him of being two-faced. The propaganda piece urges people to vote against the Liberal Party as they 'pose as champions of the constitution but deny constitutional liberty to women'. (LSE Library. No restrictions, via Wikimedia Commons)

A WSPU poster (*c*.1913) denouncing the Cat and Mouse Act and urging people to vote against the Liberal Party. (Schlesinger Library, RIAS, Harvard University. No restrictions, via Wikimedia Commons)

Right: Policemen attack a suffragette while she is on the ground during the Black Friday protest of 18 November 1910. The picture appeared in the *Daily Mirror* the next day, which stated the woman was Ada Wright, who was around 50 years old at the time. (Victor Consolé (probably 1886 – 1941), the London News Agency Photos Ltd. Public domain, via Wikimedia Commons)

Below: The Suffragette that Knew Jiu-Jitsu, drawn by Arthur Wallis Mills and published in Punch Magazine in 1910. The poster depicts Edith Garrud, the martial arts teacher to the Bodyguard. (Arthur Wallis Mills. Public domain, via Wikimedia Commons)

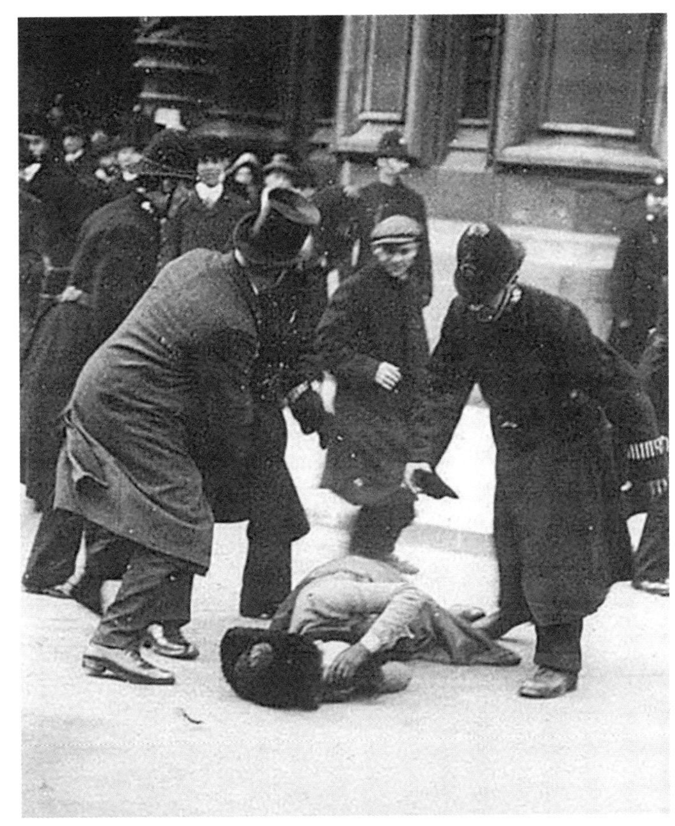

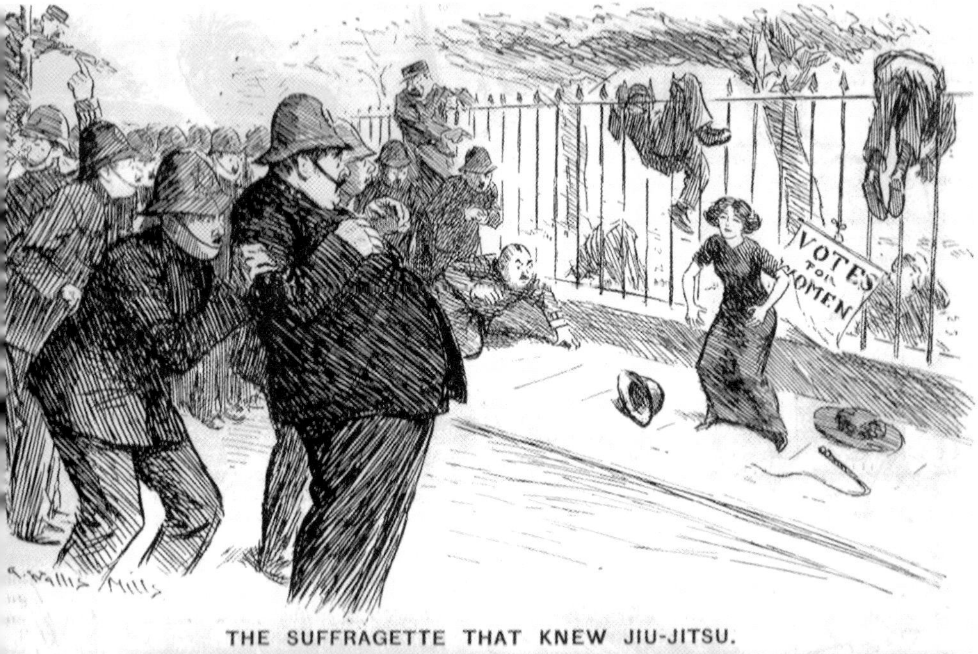

THE SUFFRAGETTE THAT KNEW JIU-JITSU.

THE ARREST.

Above: Charlotte Despard leads the Women's Freedom League at the Women's Coronation Procession on 17 June 1911. (LSE Library. No restrictions, via Wikimedia Commons)

Left: An anti-suffrage postcard by Reg Carter depicting a woman dressed in suffragette colours (white, purple and green), smashing windows (*c.*1911 – 1914). The inscription reads, 'suffragettes get wilder daily & smash shop windows oh! So gaily.' (Reg Carter (died in 1949). Public domain, via Wikimedia Commons)

Fred and Emmeline Pethick-Lawrence, (right and second right) along with Emmeline Pankhurst in the dock in 1912 at Bow Street Court for the preliminary hearing of their conspiracy trial. Mabel Tuke is also pictured (furthest from the camara) but was dismissed from the trial soon after. (LSE Library. No restrictions, via Wikimedia Commons)

Fred and Emmeline Pethick-Lawrence arriving to attend their conspiracy trial. They were driven to the Old Baily by the WSPU chauffeur Vera Holme. (LSE Library. No restrictions, via Wikimedia Commons)

Millicent Garrett Fawcett during the NUWSS march known as the Pilgrimage at Hyde Park in 1913. (LSE Library. No restrictions, via Wikimedia Commons)

Emily Wilding Davison after being struck by King George's horse, Anmer on 4 June 1913 at the Epsom Derby. Davison was knocked unconscious and died four days later. (Arthur Barrett. Public domain, via Wikimedia Commons)

A cartoon from *Punch Magazine* from November 1913 depicting two suffragettes discussing a planned arson attack. (*Punch Magazine*. Public domain, via Wikimedia Commons)

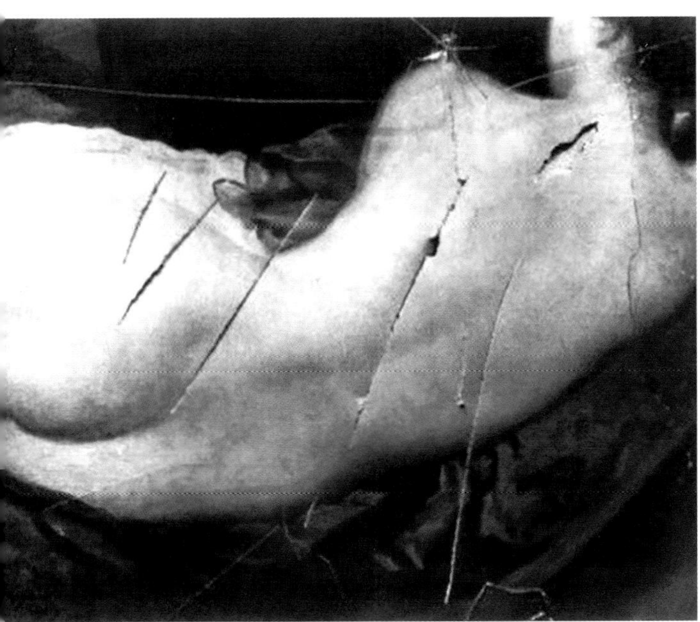

A picture of the *Rokeby Venus* that was released to the press on 11 March 1914 showing the damage done to it by 'Slasher' Mary Richardson the previous day. (Diego Velázquez. Public domain, via Wikimedia Commons)

Left: Photographs depicting the Britannia Pavilion on the pier in Great Yarmouth before and after it was bombed by Evaline Hilda Burkitt and Florence Tunks in 1914. (Unknown author. Public domain, via Wikimedia Commons)

Below: A set of surveillance photographs (*c*.1914) taken by Special Branch detectives who were watching the more militant suffragettes, in particular those involved in the WSPU's arson campaign. Featured in this picture are: 11. Mary Richardson, 12. Lilian Lenton, 13. Kitty Marion, 14. Lillian Forrester, 15. Miss Johansson, 16. Clara Elizabeth Giveen, 17. Jennie Baines, and 18. Miriam Pratt. (UK Government's Criminal Record Office (*c*.1914). Public domain, via Wikimedia Commons)

cause. I determined that if it were necessary to go to prison under another name, I should take the name of Warburton. When I went to Newcastle, my family raised no objection. Now nobody was to know of my disguise, but Warburton was too distinguished a name; that would at once attract attention. I must leave out the 'bur' and make it 'Warton.' 'Jane' was the name of Joan of Arc (for Jeanne is more often translated into 'Jane' than 'Joan') and would bring me comfort in distress …

I accomplished my disguise in Manchester, going to a different shop for every part of it, for safety's sake. I had noticed several times while I was in prison that prisoners of unprepossessing appearance obtained least favour, so I was determined to put ugliness to the test. I had my hair cut short and parted, in early Victorian fashion, in smooth bands down the side of my face. This, combined with the resentful bristles of my newly-cut back hair, produced a curious effect. I wished to bleach my hair as well, but the hairdresser refused point-blank to do this, and the stuff that I bought for the purpose at the chemist's proved quite ineffective.

A tweed hat, a long green cloth coat, which I purchased for 8s. 6d., a woollen scarf and woollen gloves, a white silk neck-kerchief, a pair of pince-nez spectacles, a purse, a net-bag to contain some of my papers, and my costume was complete. I had removed my own initials from my underclothing, and bought the ready-made initials 'J.W.' to sew on in their stead, but to my regret I had not time to achieve this finishing touch … Before leaving Manchester I realised that my ugly disguise was a success. I was an object of the greatest derision to street-boys, and shop-girls could hardly keep their countenances while serving me.

Constance Lytton. Prisons and Prisoners: Some Personal Experiences.
William Heinemann (1914).

The *Daily Telegraph* reported on 25 January 1910:

> Her ladyship said her object in courting arrest at Liverpool was to test the accuracy of [Home Secretary Herbert John Gladstone's] statement that no distinction was made among suffragist prisoners based on class difference … Lady Constance Lytton, who had previously been released from Newcastle Gaol on the grounds that she suffered from a weak heart and that forcible feeding might have grave consequences, stated that on this occasion no effort was made to test her heart … Up to Saturday the Liverpool gaol authorities had no idea that 'Jane Wharton' (sic) was other than the poor seamstress she had got up to resemble – Lady Constance Lytton was released on grounds of health. She alleges, however, that the decision was not arrived at until her identity had become known. She further states that the prison doctor, who saw her on the Wednesday evening during the forcible feeding, said, 'heart famous; pulse steady; go along; it's all right.'

A Prison Commissioner's Report to the Home Office on the incident denied Lytton's accusations:

> Such allegations, if made by an ordinary prisoner on discharge … would not be deemed to call for any further action by the Secretary of State, and any exceptional action would not … be justified by the mere fact that in this case the discharged prisoner is a women of gentle birth, highly educated, and thus enabled to make public her alleged grievances through the medium of the press and of her influential friends.

She went to Eagle House to recuperate after her bouts of force-feeding and told her story to the Blathwayts. Emily was not impressed, however, and stated in her diary, 'when the cause becomes the fashion, we shall have the stupid people in it'. Lytton's health got worse through 1910 and in August, she suffered a heart attack and had several strokes which left her paralysed on the right side of her body. She was again imprisoned for breaking windows in November 1911, although this time she was treated much better. She wrote, 'All was civility; it was unrecognisable from the first time I had been there.' She continued to support the cause by writing about her experiences and spoke about them on many occasions, and it is believed that her speeches, letters and articles helped end the practice of force-feeding suffragettes. With the outbreak of war in 1914, she turned her attention to helping Marie Stopes establish birth control centres. Lady Constance Lytton remained in ill health until she died in 1923, when she was buried with a purple, white and green cloth covering her coffin.

Sophia Duleep Singh – The Indian Princess

For women of colour, involvement in the suffrage movement often meant having to deal with racism, not only from their opponents but also from the white women alongside whom they were fighting. The record for non-white campaigners is more complete in the United States, which could be the case for several reasons. Throughout the years the suffrage movements were active, people of colour made up a smaller percentage of the population of Britain than they did in the USA (though this would change after the Second World War). Census records in the UK from the time are also unable to define the ethnicity of the people they document, so it's possible that non-white women were more active in the movement than current records show. There are, however, some instances of people of colour who were known to be involved with the movement, one of the most influential being Princess Sophia Duleep Singh (1876–1948). Despite her Indian heritage, Duleep Singh was born in London and grew up in great affluence at Elveden Hall in Suffolk with her parents, five siblings and nineteen domestic staff members, including cooks, maids and valets.

Her father was the last Maharaja of the Sikh Empire, who was exiled to Britain at the age of 15 after being forced to abdicate his kingdom to the East India Company. He became good friends with Prince Albert and Queen Victoria, who would go on to become godparents to several of his children, including Sophia and her sister Catherine Hilda Duleep Singh, who was a member of the NUWSS. Sophia's mother, Bamba Müller, was half German and half Ethiopian, and died of typhoid after contracting it from Sophia in 1887; in 1893, Sophia's father also passed away. He left a substantial inheritance for his children, on top of which, Sophia and her sisters were given an apartment at Hampton Court by Queen Victoria, where they were allowed to live free of charge, along with an allowance of £200 a year to maintain it.

She would have been considered a modern and progressive woman for her time and was well-known in socialite circles. She liked to wear fashionable dresses, attend the most glamorous parties, raise championship dogs and smoke cigarettes, in addition to which she had many trendy interests, including photography and cycling. She visited India in 1907, where she learned about the extreme poverty in the country and discovered more about what her family had lost when they surrendered to the British. Despite the luxury in which the family lived and the closeness to royalty they maintained, members of the establishment were always somewhat suspicious of the Duleep Singhs, and they were kept under surveillance by the India Office. British agents constantly shadowed Sophia during her Indian trip, but this did not deter her from learning about the cause of Indian independence, for which she had great sympathy. When she returned from India in 1909, she had gained a deeper understanding of the struggles of those less fortunate than herself and a better grasp of the day's political climate. As a result, at the age of 33, Duleep Singh joined the WSPU.

As a wealthy woman, she was able to help fund the organisation, aid some of the fundraising efforts, and contribute in other ways such as when she loaned the Kingston and District branch a trap (a type of carriage designed to be pulled by a horse). The fact that a leading member of the suffragette cause came from royalty served as an embarrassment to the government, with King George V reportedly once asking in response to her exploits, 'Have we no hold over her?' The simple answer to his question was 'no'; her status made her highly newsworthy, which aided the propaganda campaign of the WSPU. However, to keep this in check, authorities were careful not to arrest or charge Duleep Singh for her involvement in protests, fearing it would boost the profile of the suffragettes even further.

On 18 November 1910, she attended Parliament alongside Emmeline Pankhurst and a group of activists to meet with the Prime Minister. When the talks failed chaos ensued and so many suffragettes got hurt that the date would infamously become known as 'Black Friday'. After witnessing the abuse of so many women, she wrote a four-page letter of complaint to the police, to which the police responded that as the women in the protest were using violence themselves, some force was necessary. Her letter began:

FARADAY HOUSE, HAMTON COURT [*sic*].
Nov 26th 1910
Princess Sophia Duleep Singh presents her compliments to the Secretary of State and begs to make the following complaint regarding a policeman on Friday, 18th November, in Parliament Square. His number is V.700. He pushed a poor, exhausted lady so that she fell onto her hands & knees & when she got up, he took hold of her most roughly and pushed her along. Princess Sophia followed at a distance to see what happened; the lady (whose name she was unaware of) was eventually released. The policeman was unnecessarily and brutally rough, and Princess Sophia hopes he will be suitably punished.

Duleep Singh and her friend Kitty Marshall jumped out at Prime Minister Herbert H. Asquith on 6 February 1911 as he left 10 Downing Street and barred his way to his taxi. Police had been aware of a suffragette presence but ignored the two women because they were well-dressed. Duleep Singh then unfurled a banner she had hidden in her fur coat, revealing the message 'Give Women the Vote.' However, much to her disappointment, she failed to get arrested, which would have given the movement great publicity.

When the Women's Freedom League organised a mass census boycott in 1911, she decided to leave her mark. While many outright refused to fill in the form, Duleep Singh wrote on hers, 'No Vote, no census, as women do not count; they refuse to be counted. I have a conscientious objection to filling in this form.' The enumerator filled in some information on the form for her, incorrectly estimating her age and assuming she was born in India. She was also a member of the Tax Resistance League and often found herself being fined but would refuse to pay. She was fined on 22 May 1911 and had a diamond ring confiscated by bailiffs two months later but when it was auctioned off, a friend bought it and returned it to her. Undeterred, she went to court in December 1913 as she did not pay licence fees for her couch, five dogs and coat of arms, and was fined again.

Although she was only involved in peaceful protests and even refused to engage in public speaking due to her shy mannerisms, she was a supporter of militant and direct action, including the use of fire and bombs, which would become a feature of the later campaign for women's suffrage. In 1913, she was photographed selling copies of the suffragette newspaper with a placard that read, 'Revolution'. The picture was taken at her home in Hampton Court. As a result, King George V was advised in a letter from Lord Crew to evict her, but since she was his grandmother's goddaughter, he felt this would not be the right course of action.

During the First World War, she participated in the Women's Right to Serve March and worked as a nurse in London, working seven shifts a week with the Voluntary Aid Detachment. In 1917 she travelled to India, where she visited Indian soldiers in hospitals after they returned from the front lines; after the war, she helped preserve the history of the cause by joining the Suffragette Fellowship. Princess Sophia Duleep Singh continued to campaign for women's rights in Britain and India right up until she died on 22 August 1948 at the age of 71, a year after all Indian adults were given the right to vote.

> We are all interested in the thing we do not possess! Mystery is always attractive … the clogs and shawl would attract not only the public but Parliamentarians, who, like all people, look forward to a change.
>
> Annie Kenney. *Memories of a Militant*.
> Edward Arnold and Co (1924)

CHAPTER FIVE

Hunger Strikes and Force-Feeding

The Prisons Act of 1898 created three categories of confinement for offenders sentenced to two years or less and not sentenced to hard labour. Most prisoners would be locked up in the third division, meaning they had to adhere to the strictest of rules. Those sentenced to the second division did not fare much better and were often treated indistinguishably from the third-division prisoners. First-division prisoners were usually debtors, from the higher social orders, or political prisoners who were exempt from prison work and did not have to suffer the awful prison food as they were allowed to have food brought in to them from the outside.

They could wear their own clothes, mingle with fellow first-division prisoners, and send and receive letters. They could also receive visitors every two weeks, more frequently than other prisoners, and could furnish their cells. Additionally, they could even hire other inmates as servants if they could afford it. When a man obstructed the police while participating in a political protest, he was usually granted political status and would be held in the first division. However, the Liberal Government denied the suffragettes the same rights and with the exception of some well-connected and upper-class WSPU members, most were held in second and third-division cells.

On 23 October 1906, 150 women marched to Parliament to demand the vote. Only around twenty were allowed in and they were chosen based on what they were wearing, with working-class women being turned away. When Prime Minister Henry Campbell-Bannerman refused to talk to them, the women began to protest, and Mary Gawthorpe stood on a settee and began to speak. She was arrested and as others took her place, they were also arrested one by one. The ten women who were taken into custody included some illustrious names from the movement: Annie Kenney, Emmeline Pethick-Lawrence, Dora Montefiore, Teresa Billington-Greig, Minnie Baldock, Adela Pankhurst, Edith How-Martyn, Irene Fenwick Miller, Anne Cobden Sanderson and Mary Gawthorpe. They were each given the choice to pay a £10 fine or serve two months' jail time in Holloway in the second-division cells; all of them chose to do the prison time.

Although the actions that led to their arrests were clearly political, the women were treated like common criminals. They were forced to wear prison clothes, had to scrub floors and spent their time in solitary confinement when they refused to follow the rules. After an appeal to MPs from Henry Pethick, father of Emmeline Pethick-Lawrence, they were soon treated as political prisoners and his daughter, along with Dora Montefiore, were released after a few days due to ill health. The rest of the women were then released after just one month due to the WSPU campaigning against the severity of the sentences. On 31 October 1906 it was announced that suffragettes would be treated as political prisoners in the future, but this was soon withdrawn once the militant aspect of their campaign really began.

Marion Wallace-Dunlop – The Original Hunger Striking Suffragette

Marion Wallace-Dunlop (1864–1942) was an artist, author and illustrator of children's books. She was born in Scotland but spent much of her life in London where she joined the Central Society for Women's Suffrage in 1900. At some point, she decided a more militant strategy was best, so she joined the WSPU, often designing the artwork and banners for their protests. She was arrested for obstructing the House of Commons in 1908, then again in the same year along with twenty-six other women for throwing stones at the Prime Minister's house. She offended again the following year on 25 June and was charged with 'wilfully damaging the stonework of St Stephen's Hall, House of Commons, by stamping it with an indelible rubber stamp, doing damage to the value of 10s.' This came after she stencilled a passage from the Bill of Rights on a wall of the House which stated, 'It is the right of the subject to petition the King, and all commitments and prosecutions for such petitioning are illegal.'

She was found guilty and sentenced to a month in Holloway Prison, after which she immediately applied to the Home Secretary Herbert Gladstone to be placed in a first-division cell as she believed she was a political prisoner and should be treated as such. She told him that she would go on a hunger strike until this privilege was afforded to her, a tactic that Christabel Pankhurst later reported to be of her own invention without taking counsel from the WSPU leadership. In the petition, Wallace-Dunlop stated:

> I claim the right recognised by all civilized nations that a person imprisoned for a political offence should have first-division treatment; and as a matter of principle, not only for my own sake but for the sake of others who may come after me, I am now refusing all food until this matter is settled to my satisfaction.

When her request was denied, she made good on her threat and on 5 July 1909, she became the first suffragette to go on hunger strike while incarcerated. In an eerie foreshadowing of what was to come, the prison guards at one point threatened to pump milk through her nostrils but it was decided that she should be released after ninety-one hours of only consuming water, as it was feared she would become a martyr if she were to die in prison. This made little difference, however, because soon after, the strategy became a mainstay for imprisoned WSPU members as a means to protest their lack of political status.

For her efforts she would be awarded a Hunger Strike medal, introduced by the WSPU in August 1909 and handed out to all subsequent members who endured the process of refusing food. Some not only rejected food but also refused to do other things that would not have been expected of first-division status prisoners, such as working and wearing prison clothes. For the first month or so, hunger strikers tended to be let out of prison early if they started to get sick from not eating, though some were sent to care homes to allow them to recuperate.

In 1910, Wallace-Dunlop became the honorary secretary of the Weybridge WSPU branch and a year later, she developed a stencilling device so that she could stencil on pavements and buildings more quickly, allowing her to get the job done and leave before someone attempted to stop her. In 1911, she participated in, and helped organise, window smashing, for which she was arrested after breaking windows at the Home Office and given a three-week prison sentence. She was so respected among her fellow suffragettes for her contribution to the cause that she was selected as a pallbearer at the funeral of WSPU leader Emmeline Pankhurst, and was chosen to look after her adopted daughter Mary. Marion Wallace-Dunlop died on 12 September 1942 at Mount Alvernia Nursing Home in Guildford aged 77.

The Beginning of Force-Feeding

A group of thirteen suffragettes were arrested on 30 July 1909, when their plan to accost Chancellor of the Exchequer David Lloyd George was thwarted by police. Most were sentenced for obstruction and faced sentences ranging from ten days to three months, all in the second division cells of Winson Green Prison. To protest the lack of political status awarded to them, they decided to follow the example of Marion Wallace-Dunlop and go on a hunger strike. When sent to the second-division cells, they set about breaking windows with the heels of their shoes and after breaking 150 panes of glass in fifteen minutes, they were moved to 'special cells' designed for punishment, which were dimly lit and devoid of furniture. The warden stated that his officers had used force to get the ladies to comply, but only as much as was absolutely necessary. However, this did not deter the women and most continued to be unruly and refused to eat.

Some of them were sent to the infirmary, where they quietened down and took food, though it was later revealed that this was the first instance of WSPU members being force-fed. The first to suffer the ordeal was Evaline Hilda Burkitt, who would go on to be force-fed 292 times between 1909 and 1914; the second was Mary Richardson, who described it as an 'immoral assault' but nonetheless would go on to have more bars on her hunger strike medal than anybody else.

The practice had previously been used in insane asylums when a patient refused to eat, but the suffragettes were the first sane people subjected to the treatment. Sir Edward Troup, an under-secretary to the Home Office, sent a letter to the Home Secretary Herbert Gladstone on 2 August 1909, stating that the governor of the prison, Dr James Scott, and his confidante Dr Donkin, the Commissioner of Prisons, were 'anxious to feed them forcibly, they are quite clear that it is medically justifiable and that it can be done with safety'. Troup fully expected this practice to be repeated as he advised that when it is necessary, a doctor should be present to ensure it is done safely. Not everyone was on board, however; Gladstone objected, believing it would garner more sympathy for the women and their movement, a sentiment that would prove to be correct over the years to come.

By September, force-feeding was common practice for hunger-striking suffragettes, though from the start, both safety and ethical concerns were being raised. On 4 October 1909, 118 medical practitioners, including fifty-two women, signed a petition to the Prime Minister protesting against the Winson Green force-feedings. Much of the press had come to see the militant actions of the WSPU with disparagement and anger by 1909. Still, the practice of force-feeding women who went on hunger strike went some way towards winning the suffragettes favour with the press, with many national newspapers considering it to be torturous and barbaric. Henry Brailsford and

Henry Nevinson both resigned as writers for the *Liberal Daily News* because their editor, Alfred George, would not condemn the practice of force-feeding. In their reasoning they highlighted the hypocrisy of denouncing torture in Russia while refusing to do it in Britain, and stated that democratic rights should be extended to both sexes.

Mary Jane Clarke – The First Martyr of the Cause

Mary Jane Clarke (1862–1910) was the younger sister of Emmeline Pankhurst and eight other siblings. Radical political beliefs ran in the family, and her father, Robert Goulden, had campaigned against slavery. Her mother, Sophia, supported women's right to vote and took her daughters to suffrage meetings when they were still young girls, which enormously influenced their beliefs. Robert's mother was a member of the Anti-Corn Law League, and his father was a part of the crowd demanding parliamentary reform at what became known as the 'Peterloo Massacre'. Clarke ran a shop along with Emmeline where they sold painted goods, and she was described as a 'decorative artist' in the 1893 census. Mary Jane married John Clarke in 1895, though the pair had separated by 1904 and she was living with her niece, Sylvia Pankhurst. Like others in her family, she was first a member of the NUWSS but then helped her sister and her nieces, Christabel and Sylvia, set up the WSPU. She was a full-time worker for the organisation by February 1906 and was present at the first meeting to be held in London.

She led a group of suffragettes to Downing Street in 1909 and was arrested and sentenced to one month in prison. Upon her release, she worked for a while in Yorkshire and then became the main organiser in Brighton, where she would often speak in public and, when heckled, had a knack for turning her opponents' words against them. In one instance she, along with fellow suffragettes Joan Dugdale and Clara Mordan, had rotten apples thrown at them by an angry crowd. Clarke escaped, but when she looked back, she saw Dugdale was being attacked, so she forced her way through the mob, taking blows the whole time, and managed to take her friend to safety. Sylvia Pankhurst stated:

> Facing the rude violence … she displayed a quiet, persistent courage, which made peculiarly large demands on one so sensitive. Exerting her frail physique to its utmost, she was grievously ill on the eve of Black Friday, and her Brighton comrades had begged her not to go.
>
> Sylvia Pankhurst. *The Suffragette Movement*. Longmans, Green and Company (1931).

Despite the concern from her friends and her ill-health, she did take part in the Black Friday demonstration where she sustained an injury. This did not stop her either and a few days later, she was smashing windows in the protests that followed. She was sent to Holloway Prison for a month, where she went on hunger strike and was force-fed. When she was released on 22 December 1910, she seemed well and spoke at a suffrage event. She travelled to Brighton to attend a meeting and then travelled back to London. Two days later she collapsed, and on Christmas Day she died from a brain haemorrhage, probably caused by force-feeding.

Emmeline Pethick-Lawrence stated in Mary Jane Clarke's obituary that she was 'The first woman martyr who has gone to death for this cause.' A few days after her death, Emmeline Pankhurst wrote, 'She is the first to die. How many must follow … [she] will have "a lamp at her feet which she has placed there for others to pick up".' The last sentiment implies that her example will show others the way to a more righteous path, and is taken from the bible, Psalm 119:105, which, speaking of God, states, 'Your word is a lamp for my feet, a light on my path.'

Mary Leigh – An Assaulted Suffragette

Mary Leigh (1885–1978) was born in Manchester and, until her marriage, was a schoolteacher. She joined the WSPU in 1906 and two years later, was arrested along with several other suffragettes, including Emily Wilding Davison, for attempting to prevent a budget meeting led by David Lloyd George. On 30 June 1908, she, along with Edith New, became the first to employ the tactic of smashing windows. After trying to get into Parliament, many of their fellow suffragettes were manhandled and mistreated by the police. During the commotion, the two ladies slipped away, took a taxi to 10 Downing Street and smashed two windows. Both were sentenced the next day to two months of hard labour for wilful damage. Both of them declared they had been forced into this action because of the suppression of women and made it clear that the fight would continue.

When they were released from prison on 22 August, they were met by Christabel Pankhurst, Emmeline Pethick-Lawrence and a large crowd of onlookers while a brass band played *The Marseillaise*, they were taken to a breakfast party in a wagon pulled by twelve of their sister suffragettes. Leigh and New were photographed outside Holloway holding up two inedible loaves of bread that they had smuggled out of the prison.

On 17 September 1909, Prime Minister Herbert H. Asquith was scheduled to discuss the budget in Birmingham. Anticipating interference from the suffragettes, women were barred from attending, and three-metre-high barricades were set up to encircle Bingley Hall, where the meeting was to be held. Mary Leigh, Charlie Marsh and Patricia Woodlock posted up on the roof of a factory next door and while the Prime Minister spoke, they hurled slates onto the hall's roof and at Asquith's car in the street below, much to the delight of onlooking WSPU members. Inside, a group of twenty male sympathisers heckled and made it difficult for the PM to be heard, the men were subsequently beaten up and thrown out of the venue.

Twelve suffragettes were arrested that day, including Charlie Marsh and Mary Leigh, who received sentences of three and four months with hard labour, respectively. As soon as the women arrived at Winson Green Prison, they went on hunger strike and a week later, on 24 September, they were force-fed, primarily via nasal tube.

Emmeline Pankhurst and her daughter Christabel learned about the force-feeding from reading a report in *The Times*. When they did, they got a solicitor and went to Birmingham only to be told they would not be permitted to see the ladies as they had not requested legal representation. A week later, Leigh would start proceedings against the Home Secretary Herbert Gladstone on charges of assault.

Mary Leigh broke the windows of her cell as soon as she arrived and was put into a punishment cell, which had a plank bed to sleep on and padded walls. Her hands were handcuffed behind her back most of the day except for mealtimes and at night, when they were restrained in front of her. When she was returned to her normal cell, she soon barricaded herself in, keeping the warders out for three hours. They threatened her with a fire hose before overpowering her and retuning her to the punishment cell. Forced-feeding would usually be done through the nose or via stomach tubes put into the mouth and passed down the throat. Mary Leigh however had to endure both and described the ordeal in a handbill published by the WSPU while she was still serving her time in 1909:

> There were about ten persons around me. The doctor then forced my mouth so as to form a pouch, and held me while one of the wardresses poured some liquid from a spoon; it was milk and brandy. After giving me what he thought was sufficient, he sprinkled me with eau de cologne, and wardresses then escorted me to another cell on the first floor, where I remained two days. On Saturday afternoon the wardresses forced me onto the bed and the two doctors came in with them. While I was held down a nasal tube was inserted.
>
> It is two yards long, with a funnel at the end; there is a glass junction in the middle to see if the liquid is passing. The end is put up the right and left nostril on alternate days. Great pain is experienced during the process, both mental and physical. One doctor inserted the end up my

nostril while I was held down by the wardresses, during which process they must have seen my pain, for the other doctor interfered (the matron and two of the wardresses were in tears), and they stopped and resorted to feeding me by the spoon, as in the morning ... The doctor felt my pulse and asked me to take food each time, but I refused.

Charlie Marsh left prison on 9 December after being force-fed a total of 139 times. She was described as being pale and thin, having lost twenty-one pounds. The same day, the case against the prison was heard. The *Daily Express* reported the next day:

> The Lord Chief Justice said he should rule that it was the duty of the governor and medical officer of the prison to take all responsible steps to keep the prisoner in health. The only question he would leave the jury was weather the steps taken were reasonable, having regard to the condition in which the woman was. The jury returned their verdict without leaving the box, that Mrs Leigh was not entitled to damages for assault.

After her 1909 hunger strike protest, she continued to be a prevalent activist for the WSPU. She campaigned in by-elections in Wales, was arrested but not charged in connection with the infamous protest that became known as Black Friday, evaded the Census in 1911, and was sent to prison for non-payment of dog tax. There was no need for hunger striking this time because under rule 243A, introduced by Winston Churchill in March 1910, suffragettes in second and third division cells were given some of the privileges afforded to political prisoners, which brought an end to hunger strikes for around two years. Leigh was also arrested for attacking a police officer in Parliament Square during the Tenth Women's Parliament, which took place on 21 November 1911, and though she denied the charges, she was sentenced to two months of hard labour.

On 18 July 1912 in Ireland, Mary Leigh and three accomplices attacked a carriage carrying Prime Minister Asquith and his family, as well as John Redmond and the Lord Mayor of Dublin. Leigh threw a hatchet at the car, missing the PM but striking Redmond causing a minor wound. Later that evening, they set out to burn down the Theatre Royal but were thwarted by the police. Despite insisting that there was no danger to any member of the public in their actions, Leigh, along with Gladys Evans, was sentenced to five years, Jennie Baines (using the name Lizzie Baker) received seven months' hard labour for her part in the attacks, and Mabel Capper was acquitted due to lack of evidence. On the 8 August 1912, the *Daily Mirror* reported: 'A defiant speech from the dock was made by Mrs Leigh, who asserted that she would fight: "I will put my back against the wall and nothing will bring me to submission."'

In prison, Leigh and Evans went on hunger strike due to their lack of political status and were force-fed after six days on 20 August. They were fed three times daily, which worked well with Evans but not so much with Leigh. She became ill, and after sixty-four days of being on hunger strike, she had lost twenty pounds in weight. Leigh was released from prison on a conditional release licence on 20 September. She had to tell the police where she was living, stay in the country and abstain from any more militant action while out of prison. Emaciated and barely able to walk, she refused to go to a hospital but agreed to medical care at the private home of schoolteacher Gladys Hazel, where she would stay. According to a report in the *Derby Daily Telegraph* on 23 September 1912:

> Mrs Mary Leigh, the suffragette who was released from Mountjoy Convict Prison last week after a hunger strike, sent a letter to a suffragette meeting in Dublin on Sunday stating that if her fellow-prisoner, Miss Gladys Evans, who had been sentenced to five years' penal servitude, is not released during the next few days she (Mrs Leigh)

would lead a march on Mountjoy Prison, and the issue would only be decided by victory or death.

Gladys Evans was let out of prison on 3 October 1912 due to ill health after being force-fed eighty-eight times. As a result of her ordeal, she had kidney problems for the rest of her life. By December, the charges against both ladies were dropped, and they were offered paid work by the WSPU, but they had to use the aliases 'Mrs Brown and Gertrude Bentley'. Mary Leigh would continue to increase her militant protests and when WSPU activities were suspended during the First World War, she felt the fight should continue. In 1916, she helped form a breakaway organisation called the Suffragettes of the Women's Social and Political Union, although the group made little impact. She later joined the Labour Party and died in Stockport in 1979.

The Cat and Mouse Act

Forcible feeding was increasingly seen as barbaric and continued to gain sympathy for the suffragettes so, on 2 April 1913, the government introduced the Prisoners Temporary Discharge for Ill-Health Act. Hugh Franklin was the first to benefit from the act when he was released on 25 April 1913. He had been sentenced for lighting a fire on a train in protest of the way suffragette prisoners were being treated. Before being let out of prison, he was force-fed 114 times, but with the implementation of the act, in principle, it was believed prisoners would no longer need to be force-fed but would be released once their weight got down to a dangerous level. The licence meant they were to stay at home or at a prearranged address for a set amount of time while they regained their health, at which point they would be rearrested.

The act was meant to demoralise the suffragettes because for those who followed the rules it meant a cycle of hunger striking, recovering, and then going back on hunger strike after being rearrested. Their recovery time did not count towards their sentence, so the process could repeat multiple times by the time a conviction was actually served. It was soon nicknamed 'The Cat and Mouse Act', a term Fred Pethick-Lawrence claimed to have come up with (though Lord Robert Cecil is often credited with coining the term), pertaining to how it mimicked a cat playing with a mouse it had caught. The act did not fulfil its intended goal as most did not stay at home after release and very few women went back to prison after they had recovered. They would recuperate at the house of a sympathiser and once they were strong enough, continue committing militant actions. Annie Kenney explained what happened when she first experienced the Cat and Mouse Act, one of the first suffragettes to do so, after being sentenced to three years in prison in June 1913 for incitement to riot:

> I had as my visitors the matron, the Governor, the doctor, the clergyman, and the visiting magistrate. They all asked me to eat and drink, but nothing would tempt me. The matron, the doctor and I became good friends. The doctor was ever so kind and did his best to persuade me to have fruit, but fruit was no use to me. 'I must be out in three days, doctor, or I'll die on your hands!' And the good doctor did not want a death. In three days, the gates were opened … Mrs Brackenbury lent us her house at 2 Camden Hill Square. We called it 'Mouse Castle'. All the mice went there from prison and were nursed back to health and prepared for further danger work … When I recovered I was rearrested.
>
> Annie Kenney. *Memories of a Militant*. Edward Arnold and Co. (1924)

Some women added thirst and sleep strikes to their refusal of food to get themselves released earlier. As a result, by the autumn of 1913, force-feeding was officially reintroduced in some cases to keep the women in prison for longer before they had to be released on a Cat and Mouse licence (though it never entirely stopped as some prison governors were loathed to let people out before they completed their sentence).

Kitty Marion – That Malignant Suffragette

Katherina Maria Schafer (1871–1944) had an unhappy childhood and her mother died when she was an infant. Her father was unloving and violent to the extent that on one occasion he killed her puppy because he did not like the fact that it was showing her affection. She was born in Germany but moved to East London when she was 15 to live with her aunt, uncle and their children. Soon after, she became enamoured with the lively, exciting world of music halls, which was the first time she felt like she belonged anywhere. She changed her name to Kitty Marion and spent nineteen years as a dancer, singer and comedian, working with the likes of Vesta Tilley and Harry Houdini.

In the music halls she would meet women who were strong and sexually liberated, unlike the demure, chaste women typically portrayed during the period, an image that reflected what was expected of women at the time by 'polite society'. Although she met many friends from diverse backgrounds and lifestyles during this period of her life, the industry was still dominated by powerful men. She was assaulted by a man she referred to as 'Mr Dreck' or 'Mr Trash', and said of him in her autobiography *Kitty Marion: Actor and Activist*, written sometime in the 1930s but not published until 2019, 'Few women forget the first time they have been assaulted. The first time someone decided they had the right to touch, to kiss, to take without asking.'

In 1893, she was fired from a pantomime called *Madcap Mavis* after rejecting an agent who made several advances towards her. While she continued to work, she was bitter about the fact that it took longer to get top-billing roles as she would not tolerate sexual harassment, though she sympathised with other women who felt like they had to accept the advances of these men or lose their livelihood.

She knew she was far from alone in her suffering and believed that a woman should have the right to be independent and still be safe in the workplace.

She walked with the suffragettes on Women's Sunday in 1908, but at first saw it as, 'quite funny, like a pantomime Grand March'. However, when she listened to what the speakers had to say, she realised that their views on enfranchisement, equality in the workplace and within the law were the same as hers. She stated, 'I recognised the other "mad women", the women who had actually been demanding changes in conditions of which I had practically only been "talking in my dream".' After this, she joined the suffrage movement, teaming up with both the WSPU and the Actress Franchise League.

Marion was in her late thirties when she participated in her first militant action with the WSPU on 13 October 1908 and would go on to be a mainstay in their more radical protests, including smashing windows, shouting at politicians, and committing arson in the ensuing years. During a visit to Newcastle where the Prime Minister was scheduled to discuss the budget, WSPU members attended the protest citing their reason for being there as solidarity with Mary Leigh and her fellow suffragettes at Winson Green Prison. Women were not permitted entrance, so most were outside the hall, although some male sympathisers did manage to get inside. Meanwhile, Kitty Marion and Dorothy Pethick (sister of Emmeline Pethick-Lawrence) were tasked with throwing stones at the windows of the General Post Office on Nicholson Street. They checked inside to ensure the broken glass would hurt nobody, then hurled their stones. Both missed with their first throw, but Marion managed to get a second shot off and shattered a window before plainclothes officers who had been following them pounced and placed them under arrest.

When told by a police officer that women may get the votes but for the way the suffragettes behave, she replied that men do not always act in a peaceful or lawful manner, yet they have the vote. When they and their fellow arrested protesters were escorted to the police station, crowds cheered for them with some chanting 'votes for women'.

They were held for two nights in 'insanity cells' until their cases were heard on 11 October 1909. Marion and Pethick were charged with the crime of wilfully and maliciously causing damage. As she had not actually broken a window, Pethick pled not guilty but stated she was guilty of trying to do it. She received two weeks of hard labour, and Marion, who pleaded guilty, received a month of hard labour; this was the first time either woman had been given a custodial sentence. In a letter to the editors of *Votes for Women* on 1 November 1909, Pethick complained about the harsh treatment she received at the hands of the prison doctors:

> Carelessness and callousness to a marked degree, characterised the treatment of the prison Doctors. It was not until within four days of my release, and when the nasal passages were very much swollen and inflamed, that the tube was dipped in glycerine to facilitate its passage and relieve the agonising pain. Furthermore, unnecessary violence was used. I complained of this to the Government Medical Inspector, who visited me on the day previous to my release – in the presence of the doctor [whose] reply was, 'Of course one was not in the best of tempers. Miss Pethick was not the first I had to deal with!'

Once they were sentenced, many of the women who had attended the march in Newcastle went on hunger strikes both to protest the lack of political status afforded to them and with the overall aim of giving the government four choices. They could either let them out after a few days and lose face, let them starve to death, or inflict the violence of force-feeding, all of which would help gain public support for the suffragettes; the fourth option was to give women the vote.

While the press was largely against force-feeding, there were some exceptions. *The Performer*, a trade paper for actors, encouraged that Kitty Marion should be kept fit during her incarceration, whether by compulsory feeding or otherwise. As a result of her militant actions being covered in the newspapers, her stage career was all but over, and she became known in the press as 'That malignant suffragette', (a title often also given to Emily Wilding Davison). She did appear at the Hippodrome in Colchester in late 1910 in a comedy sketch called 'The King of Sleep Land', but because of the notoriety attached to her name, she used the pseudonym Miss Marie Lea.

During her imprisonment in 1909, Marion would be force-fed through both the nose and the stomach and would endure the procedure at least 232 times, sometimes three times a day. After her first experience, she returned to her cell and gnawed through her pillow to reach the stuffing inside. She then tore a page out of a bible, broke her gas lamp and set her cell on fire. This caused her to pass out, but she was dragged out of her cell by a prison guard. A couple of days later a matron fed her milk from a feeding cup, which she was in no condition to resist, nor could she face another round of force-feeding at this time.

When she left prison on 1 November, she was weak and unable to look for any acting work. However, she received letters from Emmeline Pankhurst and the Pethick-Lawrences thanking her and congratulating her on her courage, which she would treasure for the rest of her life. Although she is remembered for her militant protests, she would also employ more constitutional tactics if she believed they would be beneficial. She was at Trafalgar Square to avoid providing her information for the 1911 census on 2 April, and afterwards went to Wimbledon Common along with other WSPU members.

Kitty Marion was arrested on 1 March 1912 for breaking the Silversmiths Association and Sainsbury's windows. She had been told to hit low down on the window, so glass did not rain down from above. Two men from Sainsbury's took hold of her and marched her to the police station. On the way, a woman asked her if she was a suffragette and when she said was, the woman replied by wishing her good luck. She was given six months of hard labour and was sent to Winson Green Prison along with twenty-three other women who smashed windows that day. While there, she went on hunger strike and was force-fed for eleven days. The first time, the doctor botched it, and after he put the feeding tube up her right nostril, she was suffocating. He tried to put food in anyway, but most of it came back up. Once it was taken out, she could hardly breathe, and deep breaths were agony for her. She described the wardress who assisted the doctor as 'tear-stained', showing she had some sympathy for Marion and the twenty other women she had helped force-feed that day.

Kitty Marion was good friends with Emily Wilding Davison, who was killed when she ran in front of the King's horse at the Epsom Derby on 4 June 1913. Four days later, Marion and another woman, Clara Giveen, set the grandstand at Hurst Park racecourse alight to honour their friend and were sentenced to three years in prison for arson. Giveen stated at their trial that as no women were on the jury, their peers had not tried them. Marion declared she would go on hunger strike and refuse to be released early under the Cat and Mouse Act. While serving this sentence, she was treated harshly, and followed through on her threat by going on a hunger and thirst strike. After five days Marion was released on 8 July in a significantly weakened state, even though she tore up the Cat and Mouse licence the prison governor gave her. Giveen was released two days later and went into hiding despite her weakened state, while Marion was taken to a suffragette nursing home to recover.

She was rearrested on 12 July after breaking a window at the Home Office and given a further twenty-one days in the second division on her sentence. She went on hunger strike again, refusing to eat or drink for four-and-a-half days before being rereleased on a two-day licence. While back in the suffragette nursing home, she was visited by two friends. One dressed herself up in Kitty's clothes and left, leaning on her friend as if weak. They got into a taxi, which was promptly stopped by two detectives who had been watching the nursing home. At this moment, a lookout gave the signal and Marion, pepped up with a dose of strychnine, escaped and caught a bus to Croydon.

From 1912, she was one of the suffragettes involved in the most militant strategies of the movement including bombing and arson. She burned down the house of conservative MP and opponent of women's suffrage Arthur du Cros. The house was empty then, but she caused £10,000 worth of damage. She kept a scrapbook with newspaper cuttings of this fire and three others she carried out in the summer of 1913. She stated in her memoirs that she did a fifth, but something went wrong. Among her newspaper cuttings were reports on a fire from the empty Seafield House, described as a 'home for the imbecilic', which was set alight and wholly gutted on 23 September 1913. Another documented the bombing of Sefton Park Palm House on 14 November. The device was made out of a hot-water bottle filled with explosives and was left on the porch of the property. Although the fuse was lit, it failed to go off. The fact that she kept these cuttings suggests she may have also been involved in these incidents, though this is not certain.

She would be arrested nine times and sentenced to prison six times between 1908 and 1914. She went on a hunger strike during five of her imprisonments and endured months of force-feeding by the prison officials. She continued to commit militant acts in the name of suffrage until she was rearrested on 6 January 1914. As she was of German descent and relations between Germany and Britain were already somewhat strained by this time, the authorities managed to get her to leave the country by accusing her of being a spy. She went to New York, where she would join forces with Margaret Sanger and help her establish America's first birth-control clinic, which would later evolve into Planned Parenthood. Kitty Marion died in poverty at the Sanger Nursing Home in New York on 9 October 1944 at the age of 73.

I am content to pay the price of victory.
(Mary Jane Clarke in a telegram not long
before her death, which was caused
by force-feeding). Sylvia Pankhurst.
The Suffragette Movement.
Longmans, Green and Company (1931).

CHAPTER SIX

Politics, False Hope and Violence – The Conciliation Bill and Black Friday

A general election was to be held in 1910, with polling taking place from 15 January to 10 February. The subject of women's suffrage was mentioned by 245 candidates in their speeches, meaning that for the first time, the cause was acknowledged as a key political issue of the day. Christabel Pankhurst believed it was the militant actions of the suffragettes that led to this, as evidenced by the continued growth and support for the organisation. By this time, the WSPU boasted, ninety-eight staff on a salary, several hundred volunteers, twenty-three branches outside London, twenty branches inside London and £60,000 in the 'war chest'.

In the run-up to the election the Conciliation Bill was proposed, which, if passed through Parliament, would give a limited number of women the vote. Soon after, it was announced by the WSPU leadership that militant action would be suspended to allow the bill to be debated by politicians. However, they continued with their 'keep Liberals out' drive during the campaigning period and targeted forty seats that the Liberals were fighting to keep, eighteen of which were lost. Many of the seats they did keep were won with fewer votes and the landslide number of votes they won in 1906 was significantly reduced. The new Parliament consisted of 274 seats for the Liberals, and 272 for the Conservatives, the Labour Party increased their seats from twenty-nine to forty, and the Irish Nationalists had eighty-two seats. As the results were so close, it was agreed that another election would be needed within a year.

Early Disappointments – A Sign of Things to Come

Under the Conciliation Bill, women who occupied business premises or a farm with a rent of over £10 per annum would be granted the vote. Women who occupied a house or a part of a house would also be able to vote regardless of rental value; however, if a husband also occupied the house and was eligible to vote, she would be excluded. This meant that, generally speaking, the bill would be more beneficial to single women and widows than it was to wives but, if enacted, it would have enfranchised around 1.5 million women. This figure would be added to the 7.5 million men who could already vote, and while it did not go far enough in the opinion of many suffrage campaigners, it was seen as a good start. The first reading in the House of Commons was a success, and on 14 June 1910, the Conciliation Bill gained a great deal of support from MPs. The Prime Minister announced in June that the bill would have a second reading in July (which it passed), but he stated there was no chance of it becoming law in 1910.

As a result, Emily Wilding Davison broke the truce and smashed two windows in the Crown Office at the House of Parliament with two chalk slabs with messages to the Prime Minister tied around them. She demanded that he give 'full facilities for the new bill for women's suffrage', and told him that his insult would not be tolerated as the suffragettes 'will not be trifled with'. A judge ordered her to pay a fine or go to prison, but before she could serve her sentence the fine was paid by an unknown person (although she was not happy about this). When asked about the action by a *Daily Mirror* reporter, Christabel Pankhurst revealed that the WSPU leadership had not sanctioned it as they were still hopeful of a peaceful resolution and the introduction of the Conciliation Bill.

The suffragettes marched on 23 July and 10,000 women made it clear they were not happy that the bill would not be enacted in 1910. Despite this, it was decided that militant action would remain suspended, and the WSPU leadership would see what Parliament would say about pushing the Conciliation Bill through. By November, Prime Minister Herbert H. Asquith had made it known that he preferred the idea of a male suffrage bill that would enfranchise many of the men in Britain who did not have the right to vote. This infuriated the leadership of the WSPU, who stated that if such a bill were passed, then the Conciliation Bill would no longer be of interest to them. They would continue to fight for the vote on the same terms as men and would return to their non-constitutional methods to achieve it.

Black Friday and its Aftermath

When Parliament opened on 1 November 1910, Asquith declared that it would be dissolved on the 28th of that month and a new general election would be held. He said that government business would be discussed in the meantime, but did not mention the Conciliation Bill. To the WSPU, this was the Prime Minister making it clear that not only would the bill not be passed that year, but the likelihood of it happening in 1911 was also extremely low. The Ninth Women's Parliament protest followed and began with Emmeline Pankhurst walking to the House of Commons, aiming to talk to the Prime Minister. Several fellow leading members of the WSPU were with her, followed by 300 suffragettes walking in groups of twelve and carrying banners. Pankhurst, along with two others, was permitted to speak to Vaughan Nash, the private secretary to the Prime Minister, but when he told them he had no authority on the matter of raising the subject of the Conciliation Bill again in Parliament, they realised they were wasting their time and went back outside.

The following events made the day infamous as the protesters were severely mistreated, so much so that the 18 November 1910 became known as 'Black Friday'. The WSPU and the police fought each other for four hours, with many women suffering violent treatment at the hands of the officers as well as from men in a gathered crowd, some of whom donned the badges of the Men's League for Women's Suffrage to disguise themselves as allies so they could get close. Some of the suffragettes also reported being sexually assaulted in the fracas, both by police and by members of the public. In total, 150 women were assaulted that day, and twenty-nine reported being sexually assaulted. Despite this, 119 women were arrested.

When *The Times* reported the incident, their reports favoured the police, noting that several had had their helmets knocked off and been scratched in the face. H.N. Brailsford, the secretary of the Conciliation Committee set up to write and push the bill through, helped to collect testimonies in a memorandum that was sent to the Home Office. The document is called *Treatment of the Women's Deputations by the Police* and is now held at the London Museum; in it, a Mary Frances Earl states:

> The scene down there was terrible. But the most terrible part to me was the disgusting language used to us by the police, who were, I understand, brought specifically from Whitechapel. In the struggle here the police were most brutal and indecent. They deliberately tore my undergarments, using the most foul language – such language as I could not repeat. They seized me by my hair and forced me up the steps on my knees, refusing to allow me to regain my footing. I was then flung into the crowd outside.

Another woman affirmed in the memorandum:

> Several times constables and plain-clothes men who were in the crowd passed their arms round me from the back and clutched hold of my breasts in as public a manner as possible, and men in the crowd followed their

example. I was also pummelled on the chest, and my breast was clutched by one constable from the front. As a consequence, three days later, I had to receive medical attention from Dr Ede as my breasts were discoloured and very painful.

As with force-feeding, rough tactics in no way deterred the suffragettes and Mrs Pankhurst vowed to return to Parliament on 21 November, then every day until it was dissolved on 28th of that month. As expected, the Prime Minister said nothing on the Conciliation Bill when he addressed the House of Commons on 21 November. As a result a group of suffragettes, including Kitty Marion, Emmeline Pethick-Lawrence and led by Mrs Pankhurst, went to Parliament again hoping to get an audience with him, which they were inevitably denied. A day later, Keir Hardie asked the Prime Minister about the bill but when the reply was non-committal, a hundred women marched to Downing Street where they managed to confront him before he was rushed from the scene in a taxi and as he made good his escape, a missile was thrown that broke the window of the car.

The police guarding 10 Downing Street were unprepared and Kitty Marion managed to throw a stone at a window, though she missed and just hit a wall. Police reinforcements soon arrived, and the women were treated harshly again. Marion was one of many women arrested, though she was released without charge. According to *The Times*, the 'Battle of Downing Street', as it was dubbed, saw hysterical women screeching and behaving in an out-of-control manner, asserting that many of the women must have been 'victims of hysteria rather than of deep conviction'.

On 23 November, Marion was arrested along with eighteen other women after trying to enter the House of Commons. She fought with a police officer, clinging on to his cape while he called her names before arresting her, though she would be again acquitted and avoided prison time. After Black Friday and the protests that followed, it was deemed too dangerous to march on Parliament and the truce was soon adhered to again on the slim hope that the Conciliation Bill would pass.

The polling stations for the general elections were open from the 3 to the 19 December 1910, and the next day it emerged that Asquith's Liberal Party had won by just one seat. By the beginning of January 1911, Emmeline and Christabel Pankhurst had given up entirely on the Conciliation Bill (though members of the NUWSS were still hopeful of its success, as were many other suffrage organisations). It seemed to the WSPU hierarchy that there was no way that Parliament would discuss it when they started sessions again, so they told *The Times* that if, as they suspected, the bill was not mentioned in the King's Speech on 6 February, the militant campaign would begin again.

Winston Churchill and the Suffragettes

Sir Winston Leonard Spencer Churchill (1874–1965) is best known as the Conservative Prime Minister from 1940 to 1945, when he led Britain during the Second World War, and again from 1951 to 1955. He was an MP for over sixty years, but early in his career he found himself on the wrong side of history when, as a member of the Liberal Party from 1904 to 1924, he campaigned against female suffrage. The Liberal Government ran Britain from 1905 to 1922, and while many of its MPs supported the idea of women's suffrage, many more, including Herbert H. Asquith, Britain's Prime Minister from 1908, did not. As a result, the WSPU launched an ongoing campaign against Liberal Party MPs, opposing them at every opportunity, especially the more outspoken anti-suffragists such as Winston Churchill.

Although not opposed to the concept altogether, he argued that, as women were the majority group between the sexes, granting them the vote was a ridiculous idea. If universal suffrage were to come about, it would lead to all power transferring into the hands of women and it would favour the Labour Party. Alternatively, if partial suffrage were granted on the same terms as men and wealthier women could vote, the Conservative Party would benefit more than the Liberals.

As early as 1905, Winston Churchill was heckled by members of the WSPU. In October that year, Christabel Pankhurst and Annie Kenney attended the Liberal Party election meeting at the Free Trade Hall in Manchester when they continually interrupted him, shouting, 'If you are elected, will you do your best to make women's suffrage a government measure?' The two were ejected from the hall and later became the first two suffragettes to be arrested for their protests. On 16 October 1905, *The Times* reported that Churchill had attempted to pay the fines of the two women to prevent them from going to prison as he feared it would give them too much publicity. He was unsuccessful in this attempt, but his assertions regarding the level of press coverage the imprisonment gave to the WSPU were correct.

After the resignation of Prime Minister Henry Campbell-Bannerman on 1 April 1908, some MPs were required to be re-elected to their seats, including Churchill. On 24 April, he stood for the seat in North-West Manchester, and the WSPU were determined to get in the way of his re-election. They held a moonlight meeting where they addressed a crowd of around 500 people, which seemingly helped, as he lost the vote to the Conservative candidate, William Joynson-Hicks. There were other reasons that the people of Manchester were unhappy with the Liberals, such as their policies on tariff reforms and immigration; the WSPU leadership, however, claimed it as their own victory.

The Liberals moved quickly and found another seat for Churchill in Dundee, where polling day was announced for 9 May 1908, and the suffragettes again did everything they could to prevent him from being elected. Mary Gawthorp and Rachel Barrett were among the campaigners, and they spoke at factory gates, hired out halls and, in the week leading up to polling day, held around 200 meetings. The WSPU were not alone, and Mary Molony of the Women's Freedom League interrupted him at a meeting by ringing a bell every time he tried to address the crowd, demanding an apology from him for making insulting remarks about the suffragettes; when he was forced to give up, she addressed the crowd in his place. Although their efforts were ultimately fruitless and Churchill and the Liberal Party retained the seat, their majority was slashed by 2,000 votes compared to the general election two years earlier. Again, other issues such as free trade, Irish home rule, and temperance, were at the forefront of the reduction in votes for the Liberals; however, the suffragettes were happy to take at least some of the credit for the decrease in their majority.

Churchill's wife Clementine supported women's suffrage in the early twentieth century, although at the time she was opposed to militancy. In her later life, she backtracked somewhat and came to believe that the non-constitutional methods employed by the WSPU were vital in winning the vote. After his marriage in September 1908, Churchill became somewhat more sympathetic to the cause, although he continued to feel that it was an unnecessary change. Officially, the Liberals were, in principle at least, in favour of women's suffrage, so to some extent Churchill had to toe the line when speaking publicly, but privately he made it clear that he would resign from the cabinet should women gain the vote.

Lady Elizabeth Balfour, sister of Constance Lytton and a supporter of the WSPU (though not a supporter of violence and vandalism), attended a dinner on 3 June 1909 where Winston Churchill was also a guest. She noted that he stated he had once voted in favour of women's suffrage but would not do so again, as they had given him 'no cause to love them'. He said the WSPU had done well at first as they woke people up, but now they were alienating people daily. Balfour countered that the large sums of money they consistently raised, along with the ever-growing membership of the organisation suggested otherwise and showed that the publicity they were getting, good and bad, was serving its intended purpose.

In October 1909, Catherine Corbett, Adela Pankhurst, Maud Joachim and Helen Archdale attended a meeting held by Churchill in Dundee, along with two male sympathisers, Owen Clark and William Carr. Pankhurst and the two men hid in the attic and threw bricks and slates at the hall's lights while shouting 'votes for women'. The other three women led a group of suffragettes outside the hall and charged the barricades that had been erected there. They battled with police for over three hours, leading to many arrests. The issue of *Votes for Women* published on 19 November 1909 stated that the women 'were glorious', but pointed out that Churchill disagreed and had told the press that the suffragettes were 'A band of silly, neurotic women'. *The Dundee Courier* reported on 18 October 1909 that the three ladies had:

> A magical effect on the mob. Surging round the women, they threw themselves against the solid wall of police. The officers fought valiantly, but were utterly helpless to stem the great human tide … Meanwhile the crowd time and again charged the police, and succeeded in reaching the barricades … The crowd in Reform Street were now incensed to fever pitch, and several ugly rushes were made to force a way to Bank Street.

On 13 November 1909, a group of women including Theresa Garnett and Vera Wentworth, decided to seek revenge for the incident in Dundee when Churchill arrived in Bristol to deliver a speech. Garnett attacked him with a horse whip shouting, 'Take that you brute.' She missed his head but did manage to hit his hat and was sentenced to a month in prison for disturbing the peace. Wentworth threw a fossil at him which had a note attached to it that read, 'Liberal statesmen are fossils and out of touch.' She was arrested and sent to prison for fourteen days, where she endured force-feeding after going on a hunger strike. By February 1910, Winston Churchill had been promoted to Home Secretary. Later that year, he voted against the Conciliation Bill and made it clear that if it did pass, he did not want it enacted that year. Edward March, Churchill's private secretary, wrote in a document marked 'Not for Publication' that the feud between Churchill and the WSPU, which had gone on for over five years at this point, had made him bitter towards them. He stated that as they had harassed him at every meeting he addressed, insulted him publicly and physically attacked him, he was unlikely ever to support the cause of women's suffrage.

After Black Friday and the protests that followed, it was believed by some that Churchill had ordered the police to be overly rough with the suffragettes that day and that he had plain clothes police officers mingle with the crowds to incite them into harsh behaviour. The evidence for this is slim and speculative, though when Princess Sophia Duleep Singh wrote a letter of complaint to the police following their actions that day, Churchill instructed that they should, 'Send no further reply to her.' He denied the allegations, suggesting that his instructions had been misconstrued, stating that he had ordered a large number of arrests to be made to get the women off the streets, and prosecutions should only be made if there were serious grounds.

Hugh Franklin was a WSPU sympathiser and a member of the Men's Political Union for Women's Enfranchisement. He was present on Black Friday and was so angered at Churchill's perceived involvement in the attacks on the suffragettes that he followed the Home Secretary and heckled him at every opportunity. On 26 November 1910, he disrupted a meeting in Bradford. He later discovered which train Churchill was taking when returning to London and boarded it with suffragette Laura Ainsworth. He pulled out a whip and shouted, 'Winston Churchill, take that, you dirty cur, for the treatment of the suffragettes.' He was promptly arrested by Special Branch officers and later sentenced to six weeks in prison. As Churchill got off the train that day, three suffragettes were waiting for him and attempted to attack him; they were also seized, but he ordered that they be released. Hugh Franklin went on a hunger strike and was force-fed, but undeterred, was arrested again in March 1911 after throwing rocks at Churchill's house.

When the Home Secretary campaigned for the December 1910 General Election, he ensured a significant police presence whenever he spoke. Women would also be barred from venues, but that did not stop male sympathisers heckling him, often getting arrested for their troubles. When he went to Dundee to give his final speech, a Scottish suffragette called Ethel Moorhead threw an egg at him and as she was being ejected from the venue, she hit the men trying to remove her with an umbrella. Churchill won his seat, but it was again with a reduced majority, with 2,640 fewer votes than in the 1908 by-election.

In November 1911, while travelling on a train with his wife Clementine, two suffragettes, Fanny Parker and Ellison Gibb, stood outside his carriage demanding a statement. According to *Votes for Women* published on 16 February 1912, he became irate as he had not slept for two days and told the ladies to go away, calling Gibb 'intolerable' and 'disgusting', and asking her if she was 'a low woman'. The next day in Glasgow as he pulled up to his hotel, the window of his car was smashed by suffragette Annie Rhoda Walker, who had concealed a rock in her muff. She received seven days in prison, but it was not the end of the troubles he faced on this trip. When he arrived back in London, Geraldine Lennox charged at him calling him 'a coward and a traitor', causing him to be rushed away in his taxi.

With incidents like this happening frequently and often in quick succession, it is little wonder that he would fear for his own safety, and that of his wife, especially in the coming years as the arson and bombing campaign continued to increase. The WSPU persisted in hounding Winston Churchill, to the extent that while he was away from home in 1913, he sent a letter warning Clementine not to open suspicious parcels or leave them unattended. He told her that she should contact Scotland Yard if she had any doubt about the validity of anything delivered by post, as 'These harpies are quite capable of trying to burn us out.'

Edith Garrud and the Bodyguard

Edith Margaret Garrud (1872–1971) was a London-based jujitsu expert who helped the suffragettes learn to fight and protect themselves. Her first introduction to the martial arts came about when her husband William, a gymnastics, boxing and wrestling instructor, attended a martial arts exhibition at the end of the nineteenth century. Soon after, the pair would train and study at Sadakazu Uyenishi's jujitsu school in Golden Square, Soho. Garrud was a slim woman who was just 4ft 10in tall, so jujitsu was ideal for her as it focuses on using the opponent's weight, strength, and energy against them and targets the more vulnerable areas on a person's body. Likewise, it would be perfect for her suffragette students as they often had to be prepared to fight the police and angry crowds of men who would, on average, be much larger and stronger than them.

The Garruds were commissioned in 1908 to give a presentation to a group of suffragettes at the Women's Exhibition and Sale of Work in the Colours, but as William was sick, Edith was persuaded by Emmeline Pankhurst to do the talk and demonstration herself. A police officer who was much larger than Garrud volunteered to help and was promptly thrown by her. According to the *Daily Mail* report on the event, he was 6ft tall and 15 stone. When he landed, he lost 'his dignity, his balance, and his helmet, whereat militant members of the audience shrieked with delight'. She was so impressive that her classes were filled with suffragettes afterwards, and by 1910 she had become heavily involved with the organisation. She began to run courses exclusively for WSPU members and she would sometimes write for *Votes for Women*. She also wrote an article for *Health & Strength Magazine* on 23 July 1910 in which she stated, 'Women using jiu-jitsu have brought great burly cowards nearly twice their size to their feet and made them howl for mercy.'

After the Black Friday protests, the leadership of the WSPU decided enough was enough and vowed that moving forward, they would need to be in a position to defend themselves. A dedicated unit was formed to protect their leaders and speakers from harassment, attacks and arrest, and was to be trained by the resident martial arts teacher Edith Garrud. Known as the 'Bodyguard', the thirty women were ready to defend their fellow members and undertake the most dangerous tasks asked of them. The Bodyguard was trained in secret locations across the capital city. While jujitsu would have been their primary focus, Garrud also taught them to use a type of Indian wooden club that would help them fight against police officers with truncheons and would be concealed in the ladies' dresses until needed. Even though the Bodyguard were formidable, they were usually outnumbered so had to be prepared to be hurt and arrested if necessary when things got physical. Edith Garrud did not get involved in any protests herself, however, as she was deemed too important to risk injury or arrest.

At the so-called 'Battle of Glasgow' in 1914, Emmeline Pankhurst was expected to give a talk at St Andrew's Hall. When she got there, it was surrounded by police, but the Bodyguard had beaten them to it and arrived the night before. Mrs Pankhurst was to be rearrested as she was out on a Cat and Mouse licence but had slipped into the venue by wearing a disguise. A Metropolitan Police Report dated 11 March 1914 stated:

> Mrs Pankhurst rushing with members of her body-guard towards the back of the platform. Other members of the body-guard, who occupied the two front rows of seats on the platform, immediately rose to their feet, and held police batons, Indian Clubs, life preservers, hammers Etc. over their heads, and threatened the police that if they attempted to approach the platform they would act. The uniform officers in front of the platform then attempted to climb onto the stage, which was surrounded with barbed-wire covered with papers and flags, displaying the colours of the Women's Social and Political Union.
>
> On the approach of the police, Mrs Pankhurst's body-guard at once took up flowerpots, water bottles, glasses, buckets of water, (which were concealed) chairs, forms and everything they could use, and commenced to assault the police. During the commotion a revolver was fired, which evidently contained blank cartridges.

A brawl started less than a minute after Emmeline's speech began and was witnessed by around 4,000 people. Around fifty policemen stormed the stage, and although the Bodyguard put up a good fight and held their own for several minutes, they were ultimately overwhelmed, and the police managed to arrest Mrs Pankhurst.

When all WSPU activity was suspended with the outbreak of the First World War, the Bodyguard were effectively disbanded. Edith Garrud returned to teaching jujitsu to the general public and faded from public life and politics. She passed away in 1971, aged 99, and although largely unknown today in martial arts and political circles, she made an impact on both by helping women within the suffrage movement and beyond learn to physically fight for themselves and each other.

Kitty Marshall – Member of the Bodyguard

Katherine 'Kitty' Marshall (1870–1947) was born to wealthy parents and grew up in Preston in Lancashire. She got married in 1896 to Hugh Finch, a doctor and the son of a vicar, but successfully sued for divorce on the grounds of cruelty in 1901 after contracting venereal disease from him after he had an affair. She married her second husband, solicitor Arthur Marshall, in 1904 and they moved to London where, by 1907, they both became involved in the fight for women's suffrage, Kitty as an activist and Arthur as a defence attorney for the suffragettes.

She is best remembered for being one of the Bodyguard and was trained in jujitsu by Edith Garrud. Being a member of the Bodyguard was not all about fighting, it was also about tactical thinking, both of which were termed 'suffrajitsu' by the press. She would often act as a 'wardrobe mistress', and would be tasked with handing out disguises. This could be to speakers at an event who were out of prison on a Cat and Mouse licence to help them avoid rearrest, or to dress others up as decoys to confuse the police and help the 'mice' make good their escape.

In her role as a Bodyguard, she often accompanied leading members of the WSPU on their escapades. She was charged with obstructing police in June 1909 along with Emmeline Pankhurst as part of a group of women taking a deputation to the Prime Minister. On Black Friday she was arrested but not charged, then rearrested a few days later in a protest that followed, when she spent two weeks in prison for throwing a potato at a light above the door of Winston Churchill's home. Later that year in December 1910, she delivered a hamper complete with food, WSPU memorabilia and a Christmas card to members who would spend Christmas Day in Holloway Prison.

She was with Princess Sophia Duleep Singh when she jumped out at the Prime Minister on 6 February 1911 and later returned with Marion Wallace-Dunlop and stencilled 'Votes for Women' on the doorstep of 10 Downing Street. When the WSPU organised a deputation to the House of Commons later that year, she was arrested again and sentenced to ten days after being accused of shouting 'charge' to incite the crowd. In that same year, she consistently showed her brazenness as she would deliver a copy of the suffragette newspaper to 10 Downing Street every week, banging on the front door four times every Friday and shouting 'Votes for Women!'

She was protecting Emmeline Pankhurst and Mabel Tuke on 1 March 1912 when they smashed windows at the Prime Minister's house, triggering the return to militancy after the WSPU gave up on the Conciliation Bill. As a result, she was sent to prison for the last time and sentenced to two months in Holloway. While there, she went on a hunger strike and, after breaking the windows of her cell, spent five days in solitary confinement in an underground cell that was 'bitterly cold'. Although she was an incredibly tough and resilient woman, this got to her, and she became depressed and was constantly crying, which led to her release on 12 April.

She was soon back in action and protecting the leadership of the WSPU when, in 1913, she and her husband provided shelter for Grace Roe, who was head of organising the group at that time and was avoiding arrest for conspiracy. She put her costume skills to work again and helped Roe disguise herself when she needed to travel to France to visit Christabel Pankhurst. Kitty Marshall was a pallbearer at Emmeline Pankhurst's funeral in 1928 and also helped organise the unveiling of her statue in Westminster in 1930. She died in Halstead, Essex, in 1947 at the age of either 76 or 77.

Edith How-Martyn and the Census Boycott of 1911

Edith How (1875–1954) was born in England and educated at the North London Collegiate School for Girls, which was founded and run by Frances Buss, an early advocate of women's suffrage. She earned a degree from Aberystwyth University and became a mathematics lecturer at Westfield College. She quit this role after her marriage to Herbert Martyn in 1899, and in the following year, she obtained a DSc. in economics from London University. She had radical opinions from a young age and was a member of the Independent Labour Party before becoming an early member of the WSPU in 1905. The following year, she was appointed joint secretary of the organisation along with Charlotte Despard and she became one of the first suffragettes to go to prison for the cause, after receiving a two-month sentence for trying to make a speech in the lobby of the House of Commons.

She later left the WSPU and became a founding member of the Women's Freedom League, along with Teresa Billington-Greig and Charlotte Despard. How-Martyn was the organisation's secretary until 1911, when she headed the political and militant department. WFL members were still perfectly willing to break the law, but largely believed the right approach to achieving suffrage for women was non-violence. How-Martyn refused to pay taxes and urged members to do likewise, and in 1911, in what was probably her most significant contribution to the cause, she organised a mass boycott of the general census due to be taken on 2 April.

How-Martyn maintained that as women were barely classed as people under the law, they should not consent to be used at the government's convenience. As they would provide the basis for future legislation, she urged members of all suffrage groups to refuse to fill in the census forms. An estimated 4,000 members of the various suffrage organisations either declined to fill the forms in, wrote diagonally on them 'No Vote, No Census', or wrote in the box marked disability 'unfranchised'.

By refusing to fill out the form, people risked a fine of £5 or a month in prison. Many women ensured they were out of the house on the day the forms were to be collected, and hundreds of women wandered around Trafalgar Square until police cleared the area. Others were let into the homes of wealthy campaigners or allies, were allowed into college halls or just spent the evening entertaining themselves by doing activities such as ice skating in Aldwych, which was packed out that night with women, including Emmeline Pankhurst once she left Trafalgar Square. No charges were brought against any of the census dodgers; in the coming weeks the government decided that there should be no prosecutions for fear of generating more publicity for their actions. *The Morning Post* reported on 4 April 1911:

> Cardiff suffragists to the number of about a hundred spent the night in an untenanted shop in the suburbs – At Bristol one party spent the night in a caravan – The 'No vote No Census' revolt appears to have been loyally supported by the Liverpool and Birkenhead contingent. They spent the night at an house in Birkenhead, 'packed like sardines', according to Miss Davis, the organising secretary, who added that for breathing purposes it was necessary to keep the windows open – A census paper had been delivered to the house, and Miss Davis took charge of it, filling in the name of a manservant on the premises, and then writing, 'No other persons, but many women.'

Edith How-Martyn resigned from the WFL in April 1912 as she was disappointed with the progress being made by the suffrage movement after the defeat of the Conciliation Bill. However, she was far from finished with politics. After the passing the Qualification of Women Act of 21 November 1918, which allowed women to become Members of Parliament, How-Martin stood as an independent candidate in the General Election a little under a month later. She was not elected, though she did go on to become the first female member of Middlesex County Council, a position she held from 1919 to 1922.

In the 1920s, she campaigned for education on birth control for working-class women, and in 1929, she was a founding member of the Birth Control Information Centre along with Margaret Sanger. She had not forgotten her roots entirely, and in 1926 she established the Suffragette Fellowship that took on the mammoth task of documenting the movement. She left Britain for Australia just before the start of the Second World War, but poor health prevented her from returning home after the war was over. She established a local branch of the Suffragette Fellowship in Australia and passed away in a Sydney nursing home on 4 February 1954.

The End of the Conciliation Bill

The Conciliation Bill was due to be read in Parliament for the second time on 5 May 1911. It was opposed by anti-suffrage groups including the National League for Opposing Women's Suffrage and the Women's National Anti-Suffrage League. On 1 May 1911, *The Times* published an article called The Anti-suffrage League and the Women's Bill:

> Inquiries have already been addressed to 94,181 women municipal voters in 76 districts, and of these … less than 15 per cent, have replied that they are in favour of the vote. On the other hand … over 38 per cent have declared that they are opposed to women's suffrage … These figures, it is urged, show that any MP who votes for Sir George Kemp's Bill will most probably be keenly resented by the majority of women in his constituency.

Despite this, 255 MPs voted in favour of the bill and 88 against it, giving it a majority of 168 votes. Chancellor of the Exchequer David Lloyd George announced on 29 May that a week for MPs to debate the bill would be set aside in the next session. While the delay was disappointing the ceasefire of militant action remained because the WSPU leadership did not want to risk ruining any chance of the bill getting through, even if the chances were slim. Protests still took place, including a march known as the Women's Coronation Procession on 17 June 1911 that drew crowds of between 40,000 to 60,000 people and involved many suffrage societies; as had been promised, it remained a peaceful affair.

Although voting results on the Conciliation Bill were positive, on 7 November, the Prime Minister announced he intended to introduce a Universal Manhood Suffrage Bill that would be discussed in Parliament in 1912. It would give the vote to the men of Britain who did not have it at the time and leave room for a future amendment to include women; understandably, the women of the suffrage movement were enraged by this. Two days later, Christabel Pankhurst announced that the WSPU withdrew their support of the Conciliation Bill and let it be known that they were ready to return to militancy.

A meeting was held at 10 Downing Street on 17 November 1911, where representatives of nine separate women's suffrage societies were allowed to speak on the subject to Herbert H. Asquith and Lloyd George. After they all had a turn, the Prime Minister told them that they should pursue an amendment to the up-and-coming Universal Manhood Suffrage Bill as he had never promised to fight for votes for women on equal footing to men, as he did not believe it would serve the good of the country. Members of the WSPU were unhappy about his statements, and towards the end of the meeting, Annie Kenney found herself face to face with Asquith. She asked him if he considered himself a statesman, and he responded that he did not know who she was. She told him that all the women of the WSPU distrusted and hated him, and when he refused to talk on the matter further she told him she would be ready to discuss it with him at all his future public meetings. On seeing the tension between the two, Christabel Pankhurst approached them, gave the Prime Minister a look of disdain and told her friend that she should not fret herself with him now as their fight would take place on public ground.

> Woman is exposed to many perils nowadays because so many who call themselves men are not worthy of that exalted title, and it is her duty to learn how to defend herself.
>
> Edith Garrud. 'Damsel v. Desperado'.
> *Health & Strength Magazine*
> (23 July 1910).

CHAPTER SEVEN

The Return to Militancy

With the perceived failure of the Conciliation Bill, militant action resumed on 21 November 1911 at the Tenth Women's Parliament. Hundreds of WSPU members and sympathisers caused havoc with a synchronised attack on government buildings in Whitehall, the homes of cabinet ministers, shops in London's West End and the offices of unfriendly newspapers, namely the *Daily Mail* and the *Daily Express*. Meanwhile, Emmeline Pethick-Lawrence led around thirty women to the House of Commons, intending to enter and protest the end of the proposed female suffrage bill. They reached their destination and waited, as the window smashers had been instructed not to start until they heard Big Ben's first chime at 8 pm.

Two hundred and twenty women and four men were arrested for charges that included smashing windows, with others arrested for obstructing and assaulting the police. Among the latter was Mrs Pethick-Lawrence, who punched a police officer in the face twice when he refused to let go of another suffragette's throat. While this was something the women were used to dealing with, the violence inflicted on them was much less severe than it had been on the Black Friday protest a year earlier. In the following month, on 15 December 1911, Emily Wilding Davison soaked a piece of cloth in paraffin, set it alight and pushed it into a post box, then did the same to two others. Although the action was not sanctioned and was initially disapproved of by the WSPU leadership, it can be seen as the start of a new level of aggressive activism. In a January 1912 edition of *Votes for Women*,

Annie Kenney wrote, 'Mild militancy belonged to the past, extreme militancy would belong to the future.'

During the King's Speech in February 1912 women's suffrage was hardly mentioned, and the WSPU leadership again made it clear that they were done with the Conciliation Bill. The NUWSS, however, held out some hope and believed an amendment to the Universal Manhood Suffrage Bill may still help move the cause forward. On 1 March, Emmeline Pankhurst, Kitty Marshall and Mabel Tuke were arrested for throwing stones at 10 Downing Street and breaking two windows. Over the next hour, at fifteen-minute intervals, 150 suffragettes smashed windows of shops and other business premises in illustrious areas such as the Haymarket, Piccadilly, Regent Street, the Strand, Oxford Street and Bond Street. The women had been given their orders in the preceding two days and were instructed to keep them secret, even from each other. Those who were to take part were sent a card and would only be allowed into the meeting place at the Gardenia vegetarian restaurant in Covent Garden after producing the invitation.

Altogether, 124 women were arrested that day, including Emmeline Pankhurst and Kitty Marshall who received two-month prison sentences, and Mabel Tuke, who was sentenced to three weeks. When locked in their cells, the women smashed the windows, banged on the bars and began singing suffragette songs as loudly as they could. Some of the ladies would go on hunger strikes and be force-fed, however, the leading suffragettes urged them to stop after ten days as they were being classed as first-division prisoners. This worked for a while, but some went back on hunger strike anyway after three months to protest the length of their sentences.

It was announced that the Conciliation Bill was to be debated by MPs on 4 March 1912, and the WSPU leadership let it be known that a great protest would be held at Parliament Square on the same day. Nine thousand uniformed and plainclothes police officers turned up only to find that a few suffragettes had gathered and were acting as decoys. Instead, around 100 well-dressed women marched down the streets of Knightsbridge, smashing windows as they went. According to that evening's edition of *The Evening News*, when a mounted police officer turned up, some of the women pulled him off his horse.

The Suicide of Lavender Guthrie

Joan Lavender Baillie Guthrie (1889–1914), often shortened to Lavender Guthrie, was a socialite and actress who performed under the name Laura Grey. Before Laura Grey became her stage name, it was probably first used as her suffragette name and was the name she gave when she was arrested, as, like many middle-class women involved in the movement, she wanted to save her family from the embarrassment of having her real name in the newspapers. She was raised by her mother as her father had died of enteric fever while fighting as a South African Officer in the Imperial Yeomanry during the Boer War.

She joined the WSPU in 1908 at age 18, but only started participating in militant campaigns when she turned 21 years old. Guthrie tried unskilled labour but found it impossible to support herself on the wages. Once she found stage work, however, she could pay her way in the world, so in late 1912 she moved out of the home she shared with her mother. First she moved to Bloomsbury, an area with a reputation for decadence, though soon after, she moved into a flat in Jermyn Street near Piccadilly.

It is not clear how many times she appeared on stage, though it was probably more than once, as the inquest into her death spoke of her first stage performance in the Lyceum Theatre's Christmas pantomime in 1912, *The Forty Thieves*. Pantomime girls would appear scantily dressed and act in a provocative manner, which led many to see them as sleazy and common, so it was considered anything but a respectable career choice at the time.

She was one of twenty-three women arrested on 4 March 1912, and was sentenced to six months in Holloway Prison for breaking the windows of Garrards, the jewellers. Soon after, she went on a hunger strike, and like many of her fellow suffragette prisoners, she was force-fed. She served around four months, and while there she wrote a poem that was published in *Holloway Jingles* by the Glasgow branch of the WSPU. She marked the poem as dedicated to DR, who may be a fellow suffragette prisoner, Dorothea Rock.

To D.R.

Beyond the bars, I see her move,
A mystery of blue and green,
As though across the prison yard
The spirit of the spring had been.
And as she lifts her hands to press.
The happy sunshine of her hair,
From the grey ground, the pigeons rise,
And rustle upwards in the air,
As though her two hands held a key
To set the imprisoned spirits free.

The experience of being force-fed had a profound effect on Lavender Guthrie, and soon after being released from prison, she quit the movement. Her life started to spiral from there as she took to drinking absinthe and using cocaine (which was legal and readily available in the shops at the time). She was found dead in her Mayfair flat at the age of 25, on 8 June 1914, which coincidentally was the first anniversary of the death of Emily Wilding Davison. She had overdosed on barbiturate veronal, a substance to which she had become addicted, and she was found next to seven empty veronal bottles along with twenty-three loose tablets. A suicide note addressed to her mother was also found, but was dated from 5 June, suggesting she had been planning to commit suicide for some time before finally going through with it. According to her mother, upon leaving prison Guthrie was 'very ill', and she probably suffered from neuralgia (nerve pain). This was brought on as an after-effect of being force-fed and is where her dependency on veronal began.

Guthrie received an allowance of £100 a year from her mother, who claimed that even towards the end of her life she 'Lived in a very self-sacrificing manner, denying herself everything.' This might explain the £1,000 she left in her will, although she would have had to spend some of her money on alcohol and drugs, so it may be that she turned to sex work towards the end of her life. This was stated in the coroner's report, as erotic photos of herself and letters from several men were found in her apartment. Furthermore, in the suicide note left for her mother, she stated, 'During this last year, I have met some very dear souls, both men and women. If you ever come across them and they speak to you of me, welcome them for my sake, even though I may have met them in bad and immoral ways.'

The coroner also discovered that she was pregnant at the time she took her own life, though it is unclear whether she would have known this or not. According to her mother, she did not care for material things or the pleasures of the flesh when she was growing up, instead, she was a spiritual-minded girl who enjoyed hard work. She also remarked during the inquest of her death, 'She was not quite a normal girl. She studied very hard and had ideas of Socialism and giving her life and all to her more unfortunate sisters.'

The newspapers saw her downfall as a direct consequence of her drug taking, her time spent in nightclubs, her stage career and her involvement with the suffragettes. In a letter to *The Times* published on 13 June, the novelist E.W. Hornung, the author of *Raffles*, brother-in-law of Arthur Conan Doyle and a friend of the Guthrie family, placed the blame for the fate of Lavender solely on the leaders of the WSPU. He stated that she was 'Erratic and wilful', but it was her time with the suffragettes whose tactics had corrupted her so that the 'thirst for sensation had become a passion and the craze for revolt had become a disease'. Guthrie had received a hunger-strike medal from the WSPU, and the coroner read a letter that accompanied the award, saying of both:

Could anything be more calculated to upset the mind of a young girl than receiving this document and this travesty of a medal? The effect was quite clear. She leaves her home, sister, and mother for a garret to earn her own living and probably devote herself to this cause. She is next on the stage as a pantomime girl. Next, we find her in the company of men who are frequenting nightclubs and taking money from them. There is no more about the suffragist movement. The girl seems to have been absolutely degraded, and from then, her whole history is one of drink, drugs, immorality, and death from her hand.

The inquest into her death found that she had committed suicide during a bout of temporary insanity. Guthrie had anticipated this in her suicide note, which stated, 'Of course, the kindly Coroner will call it temporary insanity, but as a matter of fact, I think this is about the sanest thing I have yet done. I am simply very, very tired of things in general.' Her mother had worried about her mental stability, and not long before her daughter took her own life, on 26 May, she had persuaded two doctors to visit her. Although they turned up expecting to find a young lady in need of removal to a mental health facility, they discovered that she was not delusional and did not need to leave her flat. Anti-suffrage campaigners agreed with the coroner and attempted to spin her death as, at least in part, caused by her involvement with the suffragettes, but members of the WSPU were no better. They also used the suicide of Lavender Guthrie to boost their propaganda campaign, claiming that her demise as a 'fallen woman' was a consequence of her leaving the movement.

The Conspiracy Trial

On 5 March 1912, the police raided the offices of the WSPU at Clement's Inn. They arrested Emmeline and Fred Pethick-Lawrence, along with Jessie Kenney on the charge of 'conspiring to incite certain persons to commit malicious damage to property'. The arresting officer was Detective Inspector McCarthy, who returned to search the premises later that evening. Christabel Pankhurst had also been marked for arrest but was not present during the raid, and soon after she fled to France to evade being detained. Emmeline Pankhurst was already in prison at this time for throwing a stone at 10 Downing Street, along with Mabel Tuke and Kitty Marshall, and would also be charged with conspiracy, so Annie Kenney would take over the day-to-day running of the WSPU and Rachel Barret was promoted to be her deputy.

They edited *Votes for Women* together and, despite suffering from seasickness, Kenney travelled to France every weekend to get content for the magazine from Christabel, and instructions concerning the campaign. On one occasion, she discussed the organisation's future with Christabel, and the idea of a community that would vote on decisions came up again, as it had when the Women's Freedom League formed after members broke away in 1907. Kenney could see that the people who wanted this had the movement's best interests at heart but, like other leading members of the organisation including Christabel, she believed it was not prudent as the WSPU was, in fact, a revolutionary organisation and everything should continue to be decided by the few people who were in charge.

Conditions in early twentieth-century prisons were bad even without force-feeding. When Emmeline Pankhurst was sent to Holloway's hospital wing due to bronchitis on 11 March 1912, the place was infested with cockroaches. She saw one on the wall and one on her bed and was advised not to let her bedclothes touch the floor. During the conspiracy trial, which began on 15 May, Emmeline Pankhurst and Fred Pethick-Lawrence defended themselves, while barrister and MP Tim Healy defended Mrs Pethick-Lawrence. Many police officers, CID and Special Branch officers of New Scotland Yard were witnesses. Testimony from Sergeant Lionel Kirchner of the Special Branch suggested that they'd had the suffragettes under surveillance since mid-1911.

After hearing evidence for five days, the jury – all of whom were men – found the defendants guilty but recommended leniency.

However, the judge ignored this and sentenced all three to nine months in the second degree, with Mrs Pankhurst and Fred Pethick-Lawrence ordered to pay for the cost of the prosecution. The women were sent to Holloway and Fred to Brixton, and all three went on hunger strike to protest their lack of political status, which they were awarded soon after due to a protest involving over a hundred MPs and celebrities such as Marie Curie (who had recently won the Nobel Prize for chemistry), and authors Romin Rolland and Upton Sinclair. Other suffragettes were not afforded the same respect, so the hunger strikes continued in British prisons. The two Emmelines were quickly released on medical grounds, but not before Mrs Pethick-Lawrence was force-fed. Her husband suffered the same fate two times a day for ten days and was released on 1 July 1912, due to his ill health.

On 17 June 1912, the Universal Manhood Suffrage Bill was introduced to Parliament with no amendment for female suffrage, and during that summer, the militancy escalated. The suffragettes started setting fire to places and using homemade bombs, as well as burning letterboxes and causing general mayhem across the country. When buildings were burned down or bombed, they would usually leave suffragette literature at the scene to help get their point across. However, most would be careful to ensure there was a limited risk of death or serious injury to members of the public. Most of the attacks took place in the early hours of the morning, but there were several arrests, which usually led to hunger strikes and force-feeding.

The Ousting of Fred and Emmeline Pethick-Lawrence

As the militancy increased, Emmeline Pethick-Lawrence (1867–1954) along with her husband Fred (1871–1961), started to become disillusioned with the organisation and voiced concerns that between the fires, bombs and hunger and thirst strikes, more people were going to start dying. They still believed in the old ways of campaigning, like writing about their demands, demonstrating and putting on large parades and marches. In August and September 1912, the

Pethick-Lawrences went on holiday to Canada and the United States. While they were away, much of their goods were seized by bailiffs to pay the costs of the conspiracy trial, but when it was auctioned off many of their friends and supporters bought their belongings and returned them. Emmeline Pankhurst advised them to take their assets out of Britain and make a home in Canada so they could not be confiscated by police again should any other charges be brought against them. This advice was not followed, however, and when they returned home they discovered they had been the victims of intrigue.

Clement's Inn had been the headquarters of the WSPU since 1906. Back then they occupied just one room, but by September 1912 they had twenty-six rooms and thirteen more at The Woman's Press at Charing Cross. In the Pethick-Lawrence's absence it was decided that the headquarters needed to be moved to Lincoln's Inn House in Kingsway, but when Emmeline and Fred visited the new headquarters for the first time they found no offices had been set aside for them. It was revealed that they were no longer welcome within the organisation because they had dared to contradict the opinions of the leadership and urge them to reconsider their violent tactics.

Mrs Pethick-Lawrence stated in her autobiography, *My Part in a Changing World* (1938), that she and her husband were shocked at being ousted from the WSPU. They believed that Christabel Pankhurst could not have agreed to it as she was such a dear friend to them, but when they met with her and her mother to discuss the matter she made it clear that she was entirely on board with the decision. Mrs Pethick-Lawrence said after the meeting, 'I never saw or heard from Mrs Pankhurst again, and Christabel, who had shared our family life, became a complete stranger. The Pankhursts did nothing by halves!'

The Pethick-Lawrences had worked tirelessly for the organisation from its conception, and they had put much of their own money into it. Among other things, they had paid for the offices at Clement's Inn and covered the costs for *Votes for Women*. Although not a member of the WSPU, Fred had also sacrificed much of his time and effort to the cause and had been publicly ostracised for his troubles on many occasions, his enemies often resorting to name-calling, dubbing him 'Mr Pathetic-Lawrence'.

Henry Devenish Harben provided financial support for the WSPU after the split. He also gave money to the NUWSS and was co-owner of the *Daily Herald,* a newspaper sympathetic to the women's suffrage cause. Mrs Pethick-Lawrence agreed to step down and refrained from getting people to take sides because she did not want to divide and weaken the movement. Despite this, many did leave at that time because they agreed that the increase in militancy was the wrong direction for the organisation and resented the treatment of Mrs Pethick-Lawrence and her husband. Others, like Annie Kenney, were torn between the two parties. The Pethick-Lawrences were like adoptive parents to her as they took her on holidays, gave her shelter, bought her clothes and mentored her. She disliked how they had been cast aside, but she adored Christabel and loved and respected what the Pankhurst family had done for the cause; ultimately, she would stick with them.

The split was officially announced at a meeting at the Albert Hall on 17 October 1912 by Emmeline Pankhurst. She doubled down and told the listening members they would use even more radical strategies and revealed that she now expected members to go on hunger strike when arrested, even if they were granted political status. The Pethick-Lawrences were not done with the fight for suffrage, so they formed a new organisation called the Votes for Women Fellowship (VWF). As they paid for *Votes for Women* they retained control of it, and so, on 18 October 1912, the WSPU put out the first edition of their new publication, *The Suffragette.*

Rachel Barrett – Editor of *The Suffragette*

Rachel Barrett (1874–1953) grew up in the town of Llandeilo in Carmarthenshire, Wales. The middle child of three siblings, she was raised by their mother, who was widowed when Rachel was just 4 years old. After attending a boarding school, she won a scholarship to the University College of Wales, Aberystwyth. She graduated with a BSc in Mathematics and Science in 1904 before working as a science teacher in Carmarthen and Penarth for three years.

She joined the WSPU in 1906, and in the following year she joined forces with Adela Pankhurst, helping her organise her visit to Cardiff and Barry. She soon proved herself an excellent orator, giving talks in English and Welsh to get more Welsh women involved in the movement. After receiving publicity for being flour bombed when speaking at a protest in Cardiff, she left her teaching job (or was forced out) as her bosses disapproved of the actions of the suffragettes. Soon after, she moved to London where she planned to study economics and sociology at the London School of Economics. Ultimately, however, she abandoned this plan and threw herself into the campaign to gain women the vote. Later in life she stated in her unpublished autobiography that she regretted missing out on further educating herself but, 'It was a definite call, and I obeyed.'

Barrett helped organise speaking platforms at rallies from 1908, and in 1909 she worked closely with Annie Kenney in Bristol. She led a group of women to talk to Chancellor Lloyd George to persuade him to support the Conciliation Bill of 1910. After the two-and-a-half-hour meeting, she correctly predicted that the Chancellor was insincere and instead was against the bill and female suffrage in general. In the same year, Barrett became a key member of the Newport branch of the WSPU, where she would speak publicly and help organise various events and meetings. She was made the head organiser for all of Wales soon after and helped arrange Emmeline Pankhurst's tour of North Wales in 1911.

In June of that year, she participated in the Women's Coronation Procession, where she dressed in a traditional Welsh costume. Not much of what she said when speaking publicly has survived, but it was usually about the general issues surrounding the cause, the lack of political status for suffragette prisoners and the way authorities treated them. By the end of that year, her reputation within the organisation grew due to her oratory skills and her ability to debate politicians, such as Lloyd George and Reginald McKenna, the Home Secretary who she met with in late 1911.

When Christabel Pankhurst escaped to France, Annie Kenney chose Barrett to help her run the organisation. In the autumn of 1912, she was made assistant editor for *The Suffragette*, even though she had little knowledge of journalism and the paper was producing over 40,000 copies per week. Like Kenney, she was in regular contact with Christabel, and the two regularly spoke on the phone. In her autobiography, she stated that when they spoke, they had to be careful what was said as their phones were being monitored, and she always knew Scotland Yard was listening in. When the WSPU headquarters at Lincoln's Inn House was raided in April 1913, she was arrested for 'conspiring to damage property' and sentenced to nine months. During the trial she stated, 'When we hear of a bomb being thrown, we say "Thank God for that." If we have any qualms of conscience, it is not because of things that happen, but because of things that have been left undone.' After being sentenced, a prosecuting barrister described her as 'a pretty but misguided young woman'.

She went on a hunger strike when she arrived at Holloway. She was let out then rearrested three times, and each time she was put back in prison she stopped eating. Finally, she fled to Edinburgh and decided to produce *The Suffragette* from there using the pseudonym Miss Ashworth, as this meant there was less risk of the paper being shut down and her being arrested. She continued to publish *The Suffragette* until the start of the First World War, after which she aided the war effort along with Emmeline and Christabel Pankhurst. She regularly spoke about employing women and became a maths teacher at a large county school, where she was one of three women and eight men, teaching 250 boys aged 10 to 18.

Barrett had been helped with the editing of *The Suffragette* by her romantic partner, author Ida Alexa Ross Wylie (commonly known as I.A.R. Wylie,) with whom she travelled across the United States in 1919, a significant feat for two women considering the roads and cars of the time. They settled in California for a while, where the 1920 census recorded them as living in Carmel-by-the-Sea, with Wylie classified as the head of the household and Barrett registered as her friend. She later raised funds for a statue of Emmeline Pankhurst and, in 1929, became secretary of the Equal Political Rights Campaign Committee. In the 1930s, she moved to Essex and became a member of the Suffragette Fellowship, helping to preserve the memory of the movement of women's suffrage in the UK. She died in a Sussex nursing home in 1953, aged 78.

The Push Back Against the Militancy

On 23 January 1913, Parliament debated amendments to the Universal Manhood Suffrage Bill that, if passed, would add women's suffrage to it. Annie Kenney and Flora Drummond went to meet David Lloyd George and Sir Edward Grey at the Treasury, leading 300 women dressed in their work clothes from the headquarters of the WSPU to Downing Street in the process. Christabel Pankhurst had met with Kenney in France and told her that she should fight the men in the meeting while Drummond should 'interest and amuse them', in a sort of 'good cop, bad cop' routine. While the meeting went relatively well, with Lloyd George vowing he and his colleagues would accept the decisions made on the amendments by the House of Commons, the Speaker of the House decided a few days later that the amendments proposed would alter it so much that it would need to be reintroduced as a new bill. Any discussion of women's suffrage was dropped from the schedule and, as usual, was pushed back to be discussed, possibly, in the next Parliament session.

As a result, the end of January 1913 saw militancy increase again. Emmeline Pankhurst said that this was the period the campaign became truly militant as they aimed to disrupt life in England to the point of making the law and the courts look farcical. Setting fire to pillar boxes was stepped up, especially in London, Croydon and York, and arson and bombing attacks now became a more regular part of WSPU policy, which meant longer prison sentences, more hunger strikes and more force-feeding. Annie Kenney wrote in her autobiography of how the mood within the organisation darkened. She now dreaded her frequent trips to France to get instruction from Christabel rather than relishing them as she once had, because she always anticipated being arrested on her way out of the country or on her way back in. Kenney made a speech on 7 April 1913, declaring that the organisation's policy was to attack property. The next day, she was arrested and charged with inciting a riot. While on bail, she went to France using the pseudonym 'Miss James', but was arrested on her return. After a raid on the WSPU headquarters, Lincoln's Inn House, on 30 April, conspiracy to incite property damage was added to her charges and in May, she was one of eight members involved in another conspiracy trial.

Much of the press and many members of the public were furious with the increased violence of the WSPU, so much so that many suffragettes were attacked or had their shops or offices attacked as a protest to their actions. The Home Office banned open-air suffrage meetings on 15 April 1913, but the ban was never enforced. When they did speak, they had to face angry crowds and the suffragettes were sometimes removed for their own safety. On 20 April a group of speakers had to be removed from Hyde Park, and a week later WSPU members, along with male sympathisers, were set upon by an enraged crowd at the same location. Mounted police had to rescue some of the women as they tried to get into a taxi, and others were attacked with sticks and pelted with horse dung.

On 17 June 1913 sentences were handed out to those arrested on the raid on the WSPU headquarters, along with Annie Kenney. They were given long sentences in the third division, and the judge said they should not be let out early. Kenney said they would have to kill her and threatened to go on a hunger strike, causing her to be forcibly removed from the court. They all went on hunger strike and were released on licence, though some were rearrested and taken back to prison soon after. Around the time of the raids on the headquarters, the Victoria House Printing Company was also raided to halt the publication of *The Suffragette*. Their managing director, Sidney Granville Drew, was arrested and charged with conspiracy. He was released with sureties of £2,000, and he had to promise not to publish WSPU literature in the future. The National Labour Press of Manchester published the following week's edition, and the manager, Edgar Whitely, was arrested and sentenced to six days in prison, though he was released immediately. On 2 May, the police raided and destroyed the typeface of *The Suffragette*, but it was still put out in abbreviated form the same day.

The NUWSS organised a pilgrimage on 26 July 1913, where women from all over the UK travelled on foot to spread the message of the more moderate members of the women's suffrage movement. Around £9,000 was raised while the five-week walk was taking place. Asquith agreed to meet a deputation of the NUWSS on the 8 August, and while it did not change anything, some believed it served as a symbolic gesture to show that the non-militant way was more likely to gain the vote for women. Meanwhile, on 27 July, around 20,000 people gathered in Trafalgar Square to hear Sylvia Pankhurst speak. Sylvia was out on a Cat and Mouse licence, so she wore a wig and a veil to disguise herself and padded her torso with newspaper for protection. When she spoke, she took off her disguise and demanded the vote for women, then urged the crowd to follow her to Downing Street.

Violence ensued and fights broke out between the crowd and the police. Sylvia was arrested along with twelve women and eleven men. She was released four days after a hunger, thirst and sleep strike. She again broke the terms of her Cat and Mouse licence on 10 August when she spoke at Trafalgar Square. She was rearrested, again went on hunger, thirst and sleep strike, and was released on licence. Once she recovered, she left the country with Norah Smyth and went to Finland, where women had gained the vote in 1906.

Annie Kenney, her sister Jessie, Mary Richardson and Ida Wylie escaped the country for France on 19 August 1913 while out on a Cat and Mouse licence. Kenney was smuggled back to Britain in the middle of September in a large wicker hamper but was later caught and returned to Holloway. She went on a hunger strike, which she described as 'child's play' compared to a hunger and thirst strike, but the staff at the prison were determined not to let her out. When she was finally released, she had to be carried out on a stretcher, but still managed to attend the next WSPU meeting at the Pavilion Theatre in London on 6 October. Despite turning up on a stretcher, she was rearrested but released later the same day due to her ill health. She went to Switzerland to recover for a few months and visited Christabel in Paris, but she was back to her activism in April 1914.

Grace Roe – The Stand-in Leader of the WSPU

Eleanor Grace Watney Roe (1885–1979), commonly known as Grace Roe, was born in Norwood, Surrey. After the death of her mother when she was 12 years old, she was sent to Bedales, a progressive mixed-sex boarding school, after which she attended art school. Roe saw Emmeline and Christabel Pankhurst speaking at Hyde Park in June 1908, and though she was impressed, she was put off joining because of the negative press the group had received over the years. Despite her reservations, she continued to attend meetings in the following months until she saw Emmeline Pethick-Lawrence speak at Queen's Hall in October, which prompted her to join the WSPU. As she did not need to work due to a large inheritance, she could commit herself to the cause full-time and began her career as a WSPU organiser in London, later moving to Ipswich.

She was first arrested in June 1909 when demonstrating at the House of Commons but was best known for her administration skills. In addition to organising meetings and marches, she helped establish the Bodyguard and would help them to plan their operations. She also helped the campaign of suffrage supporter George Lansbury in the Bromley and Bow by-election in 1912. Lansbury lost to a Conservative opponent who campaigned on the slogan 'No Petticoat Government', and in her book *The Suffrage Movement* (1931), Sylvia

Pankhurst blamed Roe's mishandled campaign organisation for the defeat. However, others, especially Sylvia's sister Christabel, held Roe in high regard.

Roe described Christabel as the apple of her eye, and there is a suggestion that the two may have been romantically involved. When Christabel fled to Paris, Roe was given more responsibilities, and when Annie Kenney was arrested in 1913, she was put in charge of the day-to-day running of the WSPU. One of her duties was to ensure *The Suffragette* was published, and after police confiscated their printer, she bought a new one with her own money. A warrant was issued for her arrest on conspiracy charges in May 1913, but she managed to evade police with the help of the Actress Franchise League, who provided her with disguises from its stage wardrobe. Authorities finally caught up with her in May 1914, prompting her to go on hunger strike, for which she was force-fed. The *Westminster Gazette* reported on 24 June 1914:

> Mr O'Shaughnessy asked the Home Secretary whether Miss Grace Roe … at the Marylebone Police court, had been forcibly fed, and whether there was danger of her health breaking down. Mr McKenna said that Miss Roe had been forcibly fed, and her condition of health was reported to be generally satisfactory. Since she had been deprived of certain obnoxious drugs surreptitiously supplied by her friends her condition has been much better.

Her fellow prisoner Mary Richardson strongly disagreed with this report. She was in the next cell to Roe and stated in the 7 August 1914 edition of *The Suffragette* that her experiences had a profound effect on her physically and mentally. 'I consider her the most injured by forcible feeding of any in Holloway … Grace suffers extremely from pain in her nose, throat and stomach all day and night, and says she feels as if the tube were always in her body.'

When Britain declared war on Germany on 4 August 1914, everything changed for the suffragettes as the leadership agreed to stop all militant activities and instead put all their resources into the war effort. As part of the agreement, the Home Office issued an amnesty on 10 August that would release all imprisoned WSPU members, including Roe. She stuck with Emmeline and Christabel Pankhurst, along with Flora Drummond and Annie Kenney, and helped them with new work such as organising the Women's War Work Procession and trying to persuade trade unions in South Wales, the Midlands and Clydeside to support women workers. After the war, she lived with Annie Kenney and her husband in Sussex until the birth of their son. Then, in 1921, she emigrated to Canada and then to America to work with Christabel Pankhurst again. In 1925, she became a social worker in Los Angeles and would later go on to open a bookshop in Santa Barbara. She stayed in touch with Christabel and was with her when she died in 1958. Roe was appointed as her literary executor and made sure her memoirs, *Unshackled – The Story of How We Won the Vote*, were published. Grace Roe died in 1979 at the age of 93 or 94.

I love freedom so dearly that I want all women to have it, and I will fight for it until they get it.

Minnie Baldock. *Votes for Women*.
Women's Social and Political Union
(1 March 1908).

CHAPTER EIGHT

The Reign of Terror

As the militant campaign intensified between 1912 and 1914, some historians suggest that the WSPU may have gone too far at this stage. Members sent vials of phosphorus through the post that would break when handled and sometimes caused severe burns to postmen. Bombs and fire were also commonly weaponised. In May 1913 alone, the suffragettes were responsible for fifty-two attacks, including planting twenty-nine bombs and committing fifteen arson attacks. The bombing and arson campaign in the years leading up to the war were unique and had never been seen before on that scale in Britain. The targets were varied and included post boxes, timber yards, cotton mills, trains, train stations, sporting venues, churches, places of historic interest, theatres, museums and even Edinburgh's Royal Observatory. The houses of prominent people who opposed the movement were also targeted, and when someone could get close enough, even cabinet members and the Prime Minister was attacked.

As they targeted public places and the private residences of several people of political importance, it can be argued that the suffrage movement has today been sanitised and romanticised, and that some of the more militant women were, in fact, terrorists. Newspapers of the time referred to 'suffragette terrorism', both WSPU members and authorities called the sustained attacks a 'reign of terror', and Emmeline Pankhurst called the militant action a 'continued, destructive guerrilla warfare against the government'. Alternatively, the WSPU can also be seen as freedom fighters. The bombs they planted were homemade and would take time to go off, giving people the chance to get away, and they went to great lengths to make sure the nobody would be hurt in their arson attempts, resulting in very few casualties from the attacks.

It can also be argued that the more injustice they faced, the more they upped their militancy. By calling a ceasefire when the Conciliation Bill was going through Parliament, they showed that they were willing to find a peaceful solution, but they also showed that they were willing to fight back when treated harshly, be it by the police, in prison or in the courts, through longer sentences. An idea of the level of injustice women faced at the time can be gleaned from a speech by Annie Kenney in court in 1912, known as 'The Right to Rebel'. In it, she questioned the justice in handing out harsher sentences for suffragettes for causing property damage when compared to men found guilty of committing sexual assault on children. She stated:

> Here we have a child of 12 years of age at Ickleton – indecent assault. What was the punishment, gentlemen? Was it three or four months of hard labour? No. The sentence passed was a fine of £2 and £2.10s costs – £4.12s for a man who ruined a child!

Emily Wilding Davison – The Mavrick Suffragette

Emily Wilding Davison (1872–1913) is well known for attempting to stop the King's horse at the Derby Stakes at Epsom, a protest that would lead to her death a few days later. What is often forgotten about her today is the fact that she was a campaigner for women's suffrage long before this. Her actions were sometimes unsanctioned by the leadership of the WSPU, which earned her the reputation of being a maverick; however, it can be argued that she was often a trailblazer, especially with some of her more militant protests.

She was born to a family from the higher social orders, but they were relatively hard up after the death of her father in 1893. She studied

English at Royal Holloway College and Oxford University, and although she was considered highly intelligent, as a woman she was unable to earn a degree. She was a governess and a teacher for ten years but in 1906, at the age of 34, she joined the WSPU. She gave up working soon after so that she could dedicate her time to her suffrage activities, although she was not actually hired as a paid organiser at this time.

In March 1909, she was arrested and sentenced to one month in prison for causing a disturbance after trying to hand a petition to the Prime Minister. That summer, she was again in jail for attempting to gain access to a hall where David Lloyd George was speaking but was released five days later after going on hunger strike. She served her third sentence of the year in September after throwing stones, and was again soon released after going on a hunger strike.

A few days later Davison, along with Mary Leigh and Constance Lytton, threw rocks at Chancellor David Lloyd George's carriage. The stones were wrapped in paper that bore the words 'Rebellion against tyrants is obedience to God', and for their troubles, each was sentenced to one month's hard labour in Strangeways Prison. She went on a hunger strike and, in a bid to prevent the guards from force-feeding her, she barricaded herself in her cell. A guard took the unusual step of breaking a window, then pushing a hose through the gap and spraying her with freezing cold water, nearly filling the small room with water in the process. After fifteen minutes, the door was broken down and she was removed but Davison managed to sue the prison and was awarded forty shillings in damages. In a letter sent to a friend in Switzerland, she described the force-feeding she had endured in September 1909, and it perhaps goes some way to explain why she would go to such great lengths to avoid going through it again:

> In the evening the matron, two doctors, and five or six wardresses entered the cell. The doctor said, 'I am going to feed you by force.' The scene, which followed, will haunt me with its horror all my life, and is almost indescribable.

> While they held me flat, the elder doctor tried all round
> my mouth with a steel gag to find an opening. On the
> right side of my mouth two teeth are missing; this gap he
> found, pushed in the horrid instrument, and prised open
> my mouth to its widest extent. Then a wardress poured
> liquid down my throat out of a tin enamelled cup. What it
> was I cannot say, but there was some medicament, which
> was foul to the last degree. As I would not swallow the
> stuff and jerked it out with my tongue, the doctor pinched
> my nose and somehow gripped my tongue with the gag.
> The torture was barbaric.

Emily Wilding Davison was often dubbed 'That malignant suffragette' by the press (as was Kitty Marion), and she was never afraid to be innovative. On several occasions, she hid herself away in the House of Commons in a bid to reveal herself at an opportune moment. In April 1910, she intended to ask the Prime Minister about women's suffrage. She began on a public tour then hid in a heating system, where she planned to stay for the night. When she left her hiding place to find water, she was discovered by a police officer and subsequently arrested, although no charges were filed against her. The same month, she finally became a paid member of the WSPU when she was employed as a writer for *Votes for Women*.

When Edith How-Martyn organised the census boycott on 2 April 1911, Davison went beyond simply dodging the form or filling it in incorrectly. She managed to hide herself in the Houses of Parliament but was discovered that night by a cleaner who locked her in and went for a policeman, though again no charges were brought against her. In an interview with the *Daily Express* published on 4 April 1911, she said:

> I just went round with a party … then they all went up
> the crypt stairs, I stayed behind the door … There was a
> dramatic moment later in the afternoon when an MP …
> brought down two women – One of the women shuddered

as she peered into the darkness and said, 'I wonder if there are any ghosts here?' If she had come one inch further forward she would have seen my hat behind the door. I held my breath, but nobody saw me … I found there were some boxes nearby, so I dragged them together behind the door, as quietly as I could and made a bed. So, I passed all Sunday. You have no idea how monotonous it seemed – I slept a little on Sunday night, but woke at five because I wanted, as soon as the door opened, to rush the House … and say, 'Mr Asquith, withdraw your veto from the Women's Bill and women will withdraw their veto from the census.'

She fell foul of the Pankhursts when she started making protests that were not only unsanctioned but also undermined the tactics of the WSPU. When the Conciliation Bill faced a setback in 1910, she broke the non-militancy agreement by smashing windows, causing the leadership to distance themselves from her as they wished to maintain the truce in the hopes that the bill could still succeed. When the WSPU returned to their militant activities after giving up on the Conciliation Bill, it was another unsanctioned act from Davison that really got the ball rolling when she set fire to three post boxes on 15 December 1911. The tactic would become common in the coming years, but at the time, it led to a falling out between Davison and the WSPU leadership. She was sent to Holloway Prison for six months for lighting these fires, where she spent much of her time in solitary confinement and was force-fed multiple times during the two hunger strikes she endured there.

Davison was one of the prisoners who went on hunger strike on 19 June 1912 after an organised bout of window smashing and the subsequent arrest of WSPU leaders Emmeline Pankhurst, and Emmeline and Fred Pethick-Lawrence. Three days later, as a protest at her force-feeding and that of her fellow inmates, she twice flung herself over a second-floor handrail on the stairs but was caught by netting below. The second time, she hurled herself from the netting down onto the staircase below with as much force as she could muster. She dived forward and suffered from minor wounds on the scalp and the back of her head, but nothing serious. Despite her complaining of significant back pain after this, she was still force-fed, and by the time she was released on 28 June, she had lost 2 stone in weight. Prison staff described her as cheerful sometimes and sullen at others, suggesting she may have been depressed or suffering another mental affliction such as bipolar disorder. But Davison herself stated that she needed to take drastic action to highlight the injustice of force-feeding. She wrote a statement that was issued to the WSPU in which she said:

> In my mind was the thought that some desperate protest must be made to put a stop to the hideous torture, which was now our lot. Therefore, as soon as I got out I climbed on to the railing and threw myself out to the wire-netting, a distance of between 20 and 30 feet. The idea in my mind was one big tragedy may save many others. I realised that my best means of carrying out my purpose was the iron staircase. When a good moment came, quite deliberately I walked upstairs and threw myself from the top, as I meant, on to the iron staircase. If I had been successful I should undoubtedly have been killed, as it was a clear drop of 30 to 40 feet. But I caught on the edge of the netting. I then threw myself forward on my head with all my might. I know nothing more except a fearful thud on my head. When I recovered consciousness, it was to a sense of acute agony.

By May 1913 she was low on money having regularly had articles rejected for publication. Her last article, 'The Price of Liberty', was written the following month in which she talks about her willingness to make the ultimate sacrifice and die for the cause if necessary.

The article was rejected at the time but was published after her death on 5 June 1914 in *The Suffragette*. In it, she wrote:

> In the New Testament, the Master reminded His followers that when the merchant had found the Pearl of Great Price, he sold all that he had in order to buy it. That is the parable of Militancy! It is that which the women warriors are doing to-day. Some are truer warriors than others, but the perfect Amazon is she who will sacrifice all even unto the last, to win the Pearl of Freedom for her sex.

On 3 June 1913, she was also rejected for a job with the Women's Tax Resistance League. The job was for a junior typist and given her education, work experience, and years of service in the suffrage movement, it was a role for which she was more than qualified. The next day, she ran out in front of the King's horse at the Derby Stakes at Epsom and was knocked unconscious. It's unclear if this was a suicide attempt or if she just intended to disrupt the event as a form of protest, but she never recovered and died four days later on the 8 June 1913. While Emily Wilding Davison was often ostracised by the leadership of the WSPU during her lifetime for her unsanctioned actions, in death she was celebrated and even hailed as a martyr to the cause.

The Young Hot Bloods

The women who carried out the most militant attacks were part of a secret group called the Young Hot Bloods (YHB). Most were under 30 years old, only non-married women could join, and they had to pledge to perform 'danger duty' for the cause. The group's existence was top secret and was only revealed during the 1913 conspiracy trial, during which County Court Judge Matthias McDonnell Bodkin read extracts from a document headed 'Votes for Women' with the subheading 'YHB'. During the case, it emerged that Edwy Godwin

Clayton, a Fellow of the Institute of Chemists and a Fellow of the Chemical Society, ran a laboratory in which Judge Bodkin stated he, 'Put his knowledge and his brain at the Union's disposal to carry out crimes and of producing the reign of terror in London.' Clayton would receive one of the harshest sentences of all the conspirators when given eighteen months, even though he was not an actual member of the WSPU or the YHBs. While the group had their supporters, many believed their motives were less than honourable and had little to do with the cause of women's suffrage. A police officer who was charged with investigating the YHB stated in an interview with the *Sheffield Evening Telegraph* on 16 May 1913:

> Curiously enough, these Young Hot Bloods are not the women who would get the vote if either of the recent bills in Parliament had gone through. They own no property and are not married women: I don't think some of them are ever likely to be. You can well imagine how incendiarism or destruction by means of bomber appeals to young women … None of them are likely to get the vote, and, personally, I am convinced that they don't care about it. What they want is the excitement and morbid satisfaction of doing something wrong … All this seems to be abetted by a few wealthy individuals, ready to stand bail, to lend a car, or give money as required.

Helen Craggs – The First Arson Attempt

Helen Millar Craggs (1888–1969) was a teacher and pharmacist who joined the WSPU in 1908 using the pseudonym Helen Millar. After two years of campaigning, she became a paid member of the organisation and succeeded Grace Roe as the organiser at Brixton, later moving on to work at Hampstead. In 1910, she was thrown down a stone staircase after breaking through a crowd to shout about women's rights to Chancellor David Lloyd George.

Craggs' mother was a suffragist who was against militant activism, but this did not stop Helen from committing what was probably the first suffragette attempt to carry out an arson attack. On 13 July 1912, she and one other woman were found by a policeman hanging around outside the country residence of Colonial Secretary Lewis Harcourt at 1 am. When asked why they were there, they said that they had been camping nearby, but the officer did not believe them and took hold of Craggs before taking her into custody. She turned up to court wearing the suffragette colours of white, green and purple. She pled guilty to 'being in the garden … for an unlawful purpose, to commit a felony, to unlawfully and maliciously set fire to a house and building belonging to Mr Harcourt'. As the house was occupied at the time with eight people inside, she was denied bail by the judge.

It was believed that the other woman was Ethel Smyth, but decades later it emerged that it was actually her niece, Norah Smyth. This was Norah's only act of violence during her time as a suffragette, and she claimed that she and Craggs knew that the East Wing of the house where they attempted to set the fire was empty. Craggs was sentenced to nine months of hard labour but was released eleven days after going on a hunger strike and enduring multiple rounds of force-feeding. Not to be outdone, after the trial Lewis Harcourt donated £1,000 to the League for Opposing Women's Suffrage. Helen Craggs married Duncan Alexander McCrombie in 1914 and had two children with him. She was widowed in 1936 and was remarried in 1957 to Fred Pethick-Lawrence, three years after his first wife, Emmeline, died.

Olive Hockin – David Lloyd George's House

Olive Hockin (1881–1936) was an author and artist who joined the WSPU in 1912 but was most active as a Young Hot Blood in the following year. She committed her most notorious act on 19 February 1913, when she attempted to blow up a house that was being built for the Chancellor of the Exchequer, David Lloyd George. Two bombs were hidden in cupboards, the first of which exploded causing around £500 worth of damage, the second failed to explode though if it had, Lloyd George believed it could have killed twelve men. As well as the attack on the Chancellor's house, she was accused of damaging an orchid house at Kew Gardens on 8 February, helping to set a fire at Roehampton Golf Club on 26 February, placing fluid in a post box in Ladbroke Grove on 12 March and cutting telephone wires on various dates.

When the police searched her home they found stones, kerosene and false car number plates. At her trial it was revealed that a bag was found at the Chancellor's house that contained a copy of the *Daily Herald* and *The Suffragette,* both of which had her name written on them in the handwriting of her local newsagent. She followed the suffragette habit of calling out the male-dominated justice system and vowed to continue to break the law until women had the power to vote, whether she was in prison or free. Judge Charles Montague Lush withdrew most of the charges against Hockin and said she was a 'Woman who in her zeal had joined in a cause which she thought was a thoroughly good cause, and she might be right in thinking so.' She was made to pay half the prosecution costs for the fire at Lloyd George's house and sentenced to four months in prison. She threatened to go on a hunger strike but agreed to do her time quietly after she was given first-division status and allowed to continue to do art in her cell.

Following the explosion at the Lloyd George's house, Emmeline Pankhurst stated in a speech in Cardiff that, 'For all that has been done in the past, I accept responsibility. I have advised, I have incited, I have conspired.' She justified the extremity of the actions of her members by stating, 'No measure worth having has been won in any other way.' Mrs Pankhurst was charged with incitement to commit arson, and on 3 April 1913 was sentenced to three years in prison but was released soon after on a Cat and Mouse licence after she went on hunger strike. *The Times* reported on the 4 April 1913:

A scene of uproar followed the passing of the sentence.
A number of women repeatedly shouted 'shame', and

in the excitement which followed the voice of male sympathisers joined in the demonstration. There were ironical cheers, and a woman's voice struck up, 'For he's a jolly good fellow' … the police, amid continued uproar and the singing of the 'Marseillaise', removed those responsible for the disorder.

Elsie Duval and Olive Beamish – Lady Amy White's House

Elsie Duval (1892–1919) joined the WSPU at age 15 in 1907, following in the footsteps of her mother Emily Duval, a member of the WSPU and later the Woman's Freedom League. She was first arrested at the Tenth Women's Parliament in 1911 along with her mother, two sisters and her brother. She went to prison for the first time in 1912 after breaking a window in Clapham Post Office and received a hunger strike medal from the WSPU. Olive Beamish (1890–1978) joined the suffragettes in 1906, aged 16, and proudly wore a WSPU badge to school. She was unhappy that her brothers could engage in political activities for the 1905 elections, but she could not and would not be able to when she was older, which made her realise that women all over the country were in an inferior position.

Duval and Beamish broke into the empty house of Lady Amy White in Egham, Surrey, on 19 March 1913. They splashed petrol in all twenty rooms and set a fire that lasted for seven hours, causing £2,000 worth of damage. In the rookery of the garden, they left messages that read, 'Stop torturing our comrades in prison', 'Votes for women', and 'By kind permission of Mr Hobhouse'. The last message was in reference to the MP for Bristol, Sir Charles Edward Henry Hobhouse, an anti-suffrage campaigner who questioned the validity of the cause. According to Hobhouse, there was limited support for female suffrage, as evidenced by the fact that women were not damaging property in the same way as men did during the 1832 Reform riots, when men were aiming to get better representation in Parliament and an increase in the number of men who could vote.

The two women were seen by a police officer leaving the scene on bicycles, and Beamish was even pulled over and spoken to because she was riding with no lights. The same two ladies are also believed to have set fire to Sanderstead Railway Station in Croydon. They were again approached by a police officer in the early hours of 3 April 1913, and claimed they were returning from a holiday. The officer decided to follow them, and when they dropped the travel cases they had been carrying and ran, they were caught and arrested for 'loitering with intent'. Upon inspection, the cases were found to contain items consistent with an arson attack, and both were charged and given six weeks in prison.

While serving their time, the Prisoners Temporary Discharge for Ill Health Act came into being, and Elsie Duval became the first woman to be released from jail on a 'Cat and Mouse' licence. She was supposed to return to Holloway after fourteen days but never did, eventually fleeing the country to Europe until the general amnesty was granted to suffragettes at the start of the war. She died in 1919 at the age of 26 of heart problems caused by septic pneumonia contracted during the 1918 influenza epidemic, though it is believed that force-feeding also contributed to her ill-health. Beamish was released on licence soon after her partner in crime but went back to London to continue her activities.

Clara Giveen and Kitty Marion – The Hurst Park Racecourse

Clara Elizabeth Giveen (1887–1967) joined the WSPU in 1910 after witnessing how the police treated their members on Black Friday. She was involved in several militant actions as a suffragette and was sent to prison for breaking windows in 1911 and again the following year. Her most infamous action occurred on 8 June 1913, when Giveen and Kitty Marion set fire to the grandstand of Hurst Park Racecourse. According to a report in the *Bexhill on Sea Chronicle* on 14 June 1913, they caused around £10,000 worth of damage and it was probably a tribute to Emile Wilding Davison, who had died four days earlier at the Epsom Derby.

After the attack, they went to the home of Dr Eileen Casey, but a police constable who had been assigned to watch the house saw them, and they were arrested the following morning. Copies of *The Suffragette* were found at the scene. After an eyewitness gave an account, and Marion's landlady identified a piece of carpet that was used to get over a barbed wire fence as her property, the two were charged with 'loitering with intent to commit a felony'. At their trial, they gave no evidence in their defence and Giveen stated, 'Until women were on a jury as well as men, no sentence should be passed upon women.' Both were sentenced to three years of penal servitude (hard labour) but were released after five days under the Cat and Mouse Act after they went on hunger strike, though Giveen would not be rearrested after she recuperated.

Lilian Lenton and Olive Wharry – The Tea Pavilion in Kew Gardens

Lilian Lenton (1891–1972) was a dancer who vowed to join the WSPU as soon as she was 21 after hearing Emmeline Pankhurst speak. She evaded the 1911 census along with her mother and was jailed for smashing windows in 1912. Olive Wharry (1886–1947) was an artist who joined the WSPU in 1909 and was also a member of the Church League for Women's Suffrage. She was first arrested in the same year for smashing windows and spent time in prison two years later for the same crime, and then again in 1912 for interrupting a meeting of Lloyd George in Aberdeen. In early 1913, Lenton and Wharry expressed that they wanted to do more than protest and smash windows, so they were introduced to each other and became a team. After committing a string of arson attacks in London, the pair were arrested on 19 February 1913, after setting fire to a tea pavilion in Kew Gardens and being caught with a bag containing a hammer, a saw, a bundle of tow, paraffin and some paper smelling strongly of tar. When summing up at Wharry's sentencing, the judge stated:

> Not very long ago it would have been unthinkable that a well-educated, well-bred young woman could have committed such a crime as that. Unfortunately, women as a class had forfeited any presumption in their favour of that kind. They knew that well-educated, well-bred young women had committed these crimes, and accordingly, it was impossible to approach the case from the standpoint from which they would have approached it a few years ago.

After being sentenced to eighteen months in prison, Wharry vowed to go on hunger strike and stated that, as there were no women on the jury, she did not recognise the justice of her conviction. It emerged that around £400 of damage was done, but the costs would be borne by two women who held the refreshment contract of the pavilion. Wharry stated that she did not know this when the fire was set and regretted that two women had to pay the price for their actions, but in war, non-combatants also had to suffer.

Her hunger strike lasted for thirty-two days and went unnoticed by prison staff. When she left prison, she had dropped from 7 stone 11lb to 4 stone 9lb. Olive Wharry was arrested eight times in total, and each time refused to eat. She kept scrapbooks whenever she was incarcerated that are now held by the British Library in London. She filled them with drawings, satirical poems, autographs of other suffragettes she served prison time with, a record of her weight loss and newspaper cuttings of her various exploits.

Lilian Lenton smashed up her cell soon after her arrest and refused to eat. After being force-fed, she was released on 23 February as she was considered too weak to go to court. The Home Secretary Reginald McKenna denied that she had been forcibly fed and stated she was so ill because of a lack of food. The truth was that she was fed by a nasal tube, and some of the food had gone into her lungs.

This caused her to collapse, and for around two hours after, she was in a critical condition with pleurisy. The WSPU believed the doctors and prison guards knew what they had done and removed her from their custody as fast as they could so that if she did die, it would not happen in the prison. The public was outraged at the act and the fact that authorities lied about it. A leading surgeon of the time, Victor Horsley, wrote a letter to *The Times* and stated:

> The Home Secretary's attempted denial that Miss Lenton was nearly killed by the forcible feeding is worthless … she was tied into a chair and her head dragged backwards across the back of the chair by her hair. The tube was forced through the nose twice … after the second introduction, when the food was poured in, it caused violent choking.

She recovered and was rearrested on 13 June after setting fire to a Leicestershire railway station. She was also arrested in October and December of the same year but was released on a Cat and Mouse licence three times after going on a hunger strike. Lilian Lenton would escape rearrests and prosecution so often, that she would earn the nickname the 'Tiny, wily, elusive Pimpernel'. The first time she was actually charged in a court for a crime was in May 1914 for 'feloniously breaking into a dwelling-house near Doncaster with intent to commit a felony and set fire to the same'. She denied that anyone could have got hurt in the attacks as she always checked to see if anyone was there, despite this, she was sentenced to twelve months in prison and then released on licence soon after.

Miriam Pratt – The Balfour Biological Laboratory for Women

Miriam Pratt (1893–1975) was a schoolteacher who was active in the WSPU by 1913 and would sell copies of *The Suffragette* in Norwich. She soon went on to more militant actions, and on

17 May 1913, she used a paraffin-soaked cloth to set fire to the Balfour Biological Laboratory for Women in Cambridge, along with a house next to it. Both buildings were empty at the time, and the arson attack was done to protest the fact that although the buildings were intended to allow women to learn various scientific disciplines, it was of little practical use to them. At the time, women could not acquire a degree at the university and after their studies, the vast majority of the students there would have no opportunity to use their knowledge.

Suffrage literature was left at the scene to let authorities know that the WSPU had orchestrated the attack. A gold watch that belonged to Pratt was also found at the scene, as was her blood. When examined, she was found to have a wound that strongly suggested she cut herself scraping out putty around a window when removing the glass pain to access the building. Pratt had lived with her uncle, William Ward, since she was 8 years old; Ward was a police officer involved in the investigation and recognised the watch found at the scene.

He confronted her, prompting her to admit her involvement and he subsequently had her arrested. She defended herself at her trial the following October. She claimed that her uncle should have cautioned her before questioning her, but the judge and Ward maintained that it was unnecessary as he was acting as a family member at the time, not an officer of the law. Ultimately, she would be found guilty based on her closing arguments in which she admitted the charges, claiming that what she did, and by extension what other members of the YHBs were doing, was for the country's good. In her closing statement, she said:

> I ask you to look again at what has been done and see in
> it not wilful and malicious damage, but a protest against
> a callous Government, indifferent to reasoned argument
> and the best interests of the country. A protest carried to
> the extreme because no other means would avail … show

by your verdict today that to fight in the cause of human freedom and human betterment is to do no wrong.

Despite her pleas, she was sentenced to eighteen months of hard labour in Holloway Prison, where she immediately went on hunger strike. After becoming sick because of the force-feeding inflicted on her, she was released and advised to take at least three months' bed rest.

'Slasher' Mary Richardson – The Rokeby Venus

Mary Richardson (1882/3–1961) was a British/Canadian writer and journalist who joined the WSPU in November 1910 after witnessing the police brutality of the Black Friday protest. She was present when Emily Wilding Davison died on 4 June 1913 and was chased by an angry mob after the incident but was given refuge at Epsom Downs Railway Station by a worker there. She was the second woman to be force-fed in a British prison and was arrested nine times, serving more than three years in prison in total. Once the Cat and Mouse Act came into play, she would go on hunger strike as soon as she was arrested, get let out on licence, then commit another crime.

Her offences included assaulting police officers, window breaking at the Home Office, throwing an inkpot through the window of a police station, bombing a railway station and arson. She described the first time she set fire to a building in her autobiography *Laugh a Defiance* (1953), stating that she was scared when she first entered the pitch-dark building, especially when her face rubbed up against a cobweb, which caused her to be 'stiff with fright'. As she had built many campfires, that part was easy for her and quickly achieved when she, 'poured the inflammable liquid over everything; then I made a long fuse of twisted cotton wool, soaking that too as I unwound it and slowly made my way back to the window at which I had entered.'

In a now infamous act of protest which earned her the nickname 'Slasher Mary', Richardson made her way into the National Gallery in London on 10 March 1914 and attacked the Rokeby Venus, a famous painting by Diego Velazquez. With the first swing of her axe, she broke the protective glass covering the painting then slashed at the painting itself seven times. The Rokeby Venus was fully restored, and Richardson was arrested and received a sentence of six months but served less than a month due to ill health. As a journalist, she understood that attacking the painting would get a lot of attention from the press – which it did, but it also caused some members and supporters to cut ties with the WSPU as they felt the attack exemplified the fact that the militant tactics had gone too far. She wrote a statement about the incident which was reported in *The Times* on 11 March 1914:

> I have tried to destroy the picture of the most beautiful woman in mythological history as a protest against the Government for destroying Mrs Pankhurst, who is the most beautiful character in modern history. Justice is an element of beauty as much as colour and outline on canvas. Mrs Pankhurst seeks to procure justice for womanhood, and for this she is being slowly murdered by a Government of Iscariot politicians. If there is an outcry against my deed, let everyone remember that such an outcry is an hypocrisy so long as they allow the destruction of Mrs Pankhurst and other beautiful living women, and that until the public cease to countenance human destruction the stones cast against me for the destruction of this picture are each an evidence against them of artistic as well as moral and political humbug and hypocrisy.

Mary Richardson stood as a candidate for the Labour Party in Acton in the 1922 General Election, as an independent for the same seat two years later, and again as a Labour candidate for Aldershot in the 1931 General Elections, but lost on all three occasions. She would later join the British Union of Fascists led by Sir Oswald Mosley as she saw similarities to their movement with that of the suffragettes but left after two years when she came to doubt the sincerity of their policies concerning women.

Evaline Hilda Burkitt and Florence Tunks – The Bath Hotel in Felixstowe

Evaline Hilda Burkitt (1876–1955) joined the WSPU in 1907 and was arrested several times, becoming the first suffragette to be force-fed in 1909, as well as having the distinction of being the last to undergo that procedure in Holloway Prison. At 37 years old, she would have been older than most members of the YHB, and she had first partnered up with Clara Giveen. The pair were arrested on 13 November 1913, for trying to set fire to the grandstand at the Headingley Football Ground, and it was not long after that Burkitt joined forces with a 22-year-old militant campaigner, Florence Olivia Tunks (1891–1985), a bookkeeper who joined the WSPU in early 1914.

The two carried out a series of arson attacks in Cardiff. Next, they went on a two-week spree of arson attacks in April 1914 in Suffolk, where they rode bicycles across the countryside and left phosphorus in haystacks so they would catch fire a little while later. On 17 April they bombed the Britannia Pavilion on the pier in Great Yarmouth, totally destroying it. The following day, *The Times* reported that the Pavilion owner had received a letter that just read 'Retribution', and a suffragette postcard was found nearby that referenced the Home Secretary, which read, 'Mr McKenna has nearly killed Mrs Pankhurst. We can show no mercy until women are enfranchised.'

The two women next travelled to the town of Felixstowe. While there, they set fire to the Bath Hotel, which was closed at the time because it was not tourist season, but they still managed to do around £35,000 worth of damage. At the scene, authorities later found labels with 'Votes for Women' written on them and a banner that read, 'There will be no peace until women get the vote.' The landlord of the room they were renting saw them near the scene when it was on fire and identified them to police, who searched their rooms and found two boxes of matches, four candles, a glazier's diamond, four copies of *The Suffragette* newspaper, a lamp, a hammer and pliers.

They were charged on 26 May with setting fire to the Bath Hotel as well as various wheat stack fires, but refused to answer any questions when in court and sat with their backs to the magistrate while the evidence was being given. While court officials were speaking, they shouted out that they did not recognise the authority of the court and that they objected to having a jury full of men, and Burkitt even threw her shoes at a Royal Navy Officer who was giving evidence against them. Hilda Burkitt was sentenced to two years in prison, and Florence Tunks was sentenced to nine months. Both ladies went on hunger strike and were force-fed multiple times before their release. In 2014, a hundred years after they burned down the Bath Hotel, a plaque was unveiled by the Felixstowe Society commemorating Evaline Hilda Burkitt and Florence Tunks on what remained of the building.

> We women suffragists have a great mission – the greatest mission the world has ever known. It is to free half the human race, and through that freedom to save the rest.
>
> Emmeline Pankhurst.
> Speech at the Albert Hall London
> (17 October 1912).

CHAPTER NINE

The Women's Movement – The Struggle Continues

With the passing of the Representation of the People Act of 1918, and again after the Equal Franchise Act of 1928, many of the suffrage organisations that fought for female enfranchisement were disbanded and most of the women who fought for the vote, be it through militant or constitutional methods, settled down into a normal life. However, the struggle for women's rights continued and many suffragists and suffragettes either joined new organisations or remained with ones that evolved into something new. Although the vote was now won, there was still a lot to fight for and some of the issues that became prominent in the interwar years were: improved maternity and infant care, health and safety in the workplace, better opportunities for women within education, and contraceptive and abortion rights, to name just a few.

The WSPU was rebranded as the Women's Party, which was meant to be a political entity that appealed to women. When they began, they intended to help the country win the war while still having a focus on women's causes, and as well as a name change they had a new slogan: 'Victory, National Security and Progress'. Christabel Pankhurst stood as the party's candidate for the Smethwick constituency in Staffordshire in 1918 and gained over 47 per cent of the vote. Unfortunately, she lost to the only other candidate, John Davison of the Labour Party, and the Women's Party ceased to exist soon after in June 1919.

The NUWSS changed its name to the National Union of Societies for Equal Citizenship in 1919, and in the same year, Millicent Garrett Fawcett resigned and was replaced by Eleanor Rathbone. They continued to campaign for votes on equal terms as men until it was achieved in 1928, after which the organisation split into the short-lived National Council for Equal Citizenship, which focused on equal rights for women, and the Union of Townswomen's Guilds, which was mainly concerned with improving education for girls, and government welfare for women.

Margaret Haig Thomas – Continuing the Fight for Equality

Margaret Haig Thomas (1883–1958), often remembered as Lady Rhondda, is an example of a suffrage campaigner who continued to fight for equality for women. She was the only child of David Alfred Thomas, a Liberal MP and businessman, and Sybil Margaret Thomas. Governesses taught her at home when she was young, and later she attended Somerville College in Oxford. She married Captain Humphrey Mackworth in 1908, but the marriage did not last long and the two divorced childless in 1922. She later wrote of their differences in her autobiography *This Was My World* (1933), 'Humphrey held that no one should ever read in a room where anyone else wanted to talk. I … held, on the contrary, that no one should ever talk in a room where anyone else wanted to read.'

Although her mother had supported the NUWSS, Margaret believed in the more militant tactics of the suffragettes. Together, they joined the WSPU procession to Hyde Park on 21 July 1908, and soon after, she decided to join the organisation. She was involved in many activities to help the cause, especially in the Newport area of Wales, where she had set up a branch of the WSPU herself. Her father supported female suffrage but was against the use of militant action to obtain it, so he objected to her joining the WSPU at first. He later changed his mind, and she stated in her autobiography that he told her, 'He could be no judge of a matter which concerned one primarily as a woman.'

In 1909, she spoke at an open-air meeting in Cardiff Docks on behalf of the Women's Freedom League. The crowd became hostile, so her father had to force his way through the mob to stand by her side. After he also received abuse, the meeting was abandoned, prompting the *Western Mail* to defend free speech. It stated on 18 November that it disliked the breaking up of meetings even though women had done 'some silly things in their advocacy of the suffrage'. On the same day as the *Western Mail* article was published, Thomas spoke in Merthyr with Annie Kenney. The crowd were members of the Liberal Party who were also hostile to them, and began throwing herrings, tomatoes and cabbages at the women on the speaking platform. From there, things got worse as live mice were set loose in the hall, along with sulphurated hydrogen gas, snuff and cayenne pepper designed to cause irritation to the eyes, noses and throats of the speakers. The women managed to escape in a cab, and the *Aberdare Leader* reported on 27 November 1909, that the meeting was the rowdiest seen in the town for thirty years.

The following week in Newport, another meeting was broken up because of an unruly crowd that hit Marion Wallace-Dunlop with a bag of flour, but it was in the following year that Margaret Haig Thomas would gain infamy within the movement. She jumped onto the bonnet of the car of the anti-suffrage Prime Minister Herbert H. Asquith, resulting in her being attacked by a crowd of onlooking men, which led to her hat being pulled off, her clothes being torn, and her hair pulled. She recalled in her autobiography when it happened, the PM leaned back, 'Looking white and frightened and rather like a fascinated rabbit.'

From December 1911, over 50,000 pillar boxes were targeted in the country and in March 1913, there were fourteen attacks in Cardiff alone. Laurence Housman, co-founder of the Men's League for Women's Suffrage, spoke of staying at the home of the Thomas family that year in his autobiography, *The Unexpected Years* (1936).

While at a dinner party there, the discussion turned to a letterbox that had been set on fire in the area that very week. Most of the guests disapproved and according to Housman, 'It was hoped that the perpetrators would be caught and punished. My host's daughter was sitting next to me: she gave me a soft nudge. "I did it," she said.'

Thomas had travelled to London and received twelve long glass tubes complete with corks, half containing phosphorus and the other half containing a chemical compound which, when mixed, would produce flames. In June 1913, she took two of the tubes to Newport to attempt to set fire to a Royal Mail post box. Although she was nervous, she smashed the two glass tubes on the inside of the letter box making it look to any passer-by that she was just posting a letter. The box soon started to smoke, so water was brought from a nearby house to put the fire out, and a postman was able to save some of the letters. Thomas was arrested the next day and was sent to prison after refusing to pay a £10 fine. After going on a hunger strike, she was released after six days under the Cat and Mouse Act and by the time the licence had expired, the fine had been paid anonymously. Like many upper-class suffragettes, Margaret seems to have been treated well when serving her time and complimented the staff of Usk Prison in *This Was My World*, all except the chaplain, who would not allow her access to books from the prison library.

In 1914, Margaret Haig Thomas joined the WSPU's support of the war, and her parents cordoned off a part of their mansion to be used as a makeshift hospital. On 7 May 1915, Margaret and her father were returning from a business trip to New York when their ship was sunk after being torpedoed by a German U-boat. As the boat was going down, the two became separated and while David managed to get onto a lifeboat, Margaret found herself adrift in the sea for over two hours before being rescued. This experience, which killed 1,198 passengers of the steamship *Lusitania*, made her more determined to aid the war effort.

In 1917, she became the commissioner of Women's National Service for Wales and Monmouthshire, where she would be responsible for recruiting women to volunteer to work in agriculture.

She also helped recruit clerical and domestic workers for the Women's Auxiliary Army Corps from 1918 to serve in France and free up male soldiers for combat. In February 1918, she became Chief Controller of women's recruitment in the Ministry of National Service in London and soon after published an article called *The Women of Great Britain*, in which she stated:

> Nothing in the whole conduct of the war has been more striking than the readiness and the ability of the women in all the belligerent nations to render invaluable service to their respective countries and nothing has been stranger than the slowness of various Governments to realise the vast capacity of the resources upon which they might draw.

When the war was over, many women were no longer needed in the places where they had been employed, being replaced by men who were returning members of the armed forces. Despite promises made during the war that women would be allowed to continue working, the only industries recognised as viable forms of work for women by the Ministry of Labour (now the Department for Work and Pensions) were tailoring, laundry and domestic service. To combat this, she founded the Women's Industrial League in 1919, which fought for equal training and employment opportunities for women in post-war Britain. She also established the Efficiency Cub in the summer of 1919, which allowed British businesswomen to network and had four main aims:

- To promote better organisation and cooperation between professional women;
- To encourage all women in the workplace to strive for self-reliance and self-governance;
- To form networks among businesswomen;
- To get the British Chambers of Commerce to permit the admission of women.

After the introduction of the Ministry of Health Act (1919), which established a government department responsible for health policies in Britain, Thomas hired a committee which primarily consisted of women, called the Consultative Council on General Health Questions. When lobbying for such a committee the previous year, she wanted it to be all female as it was particularly concerned with maternity and infant welfare.

She founded a weekly journal called *Time and Tide*, which focused on feminist issues in politics, economics, social issues and the arts, and published works by George Orwell, Virginia Woolf, JRR Tolkien, Olive Schreiner, and many other writers. The board of *Time and Tide* were all-female, as were the in-house writers and editor. The first editor was Helen Archdale, who had previously been an editor on *The Suffragette* and was probably Thomas's lover. From 1926, Thomas edited the paper herself and continued to do so for the rest of her life. The readership was a mixture of men and women who could read about women's issues that were being fought for, and the victories that the various arms of the women's movement had won over the years. These would include women being elected to Parliament, the appointment of women as magistrates and as jury members, and the granting of degrees to women at universities such as Oxford, but the journal also dealt with issues that went beyond the women's movement. She wrote in the first issue of *Time and Tide* on 14 May 1920, 'There is another need in our press of which the average person of today is conscious, but which must specially weigh with women – the lack of a paper which shall treat men and women as equally part of the great human family.'

In the early years the newspaper tended to be more left-leaning politically, but by 1931, with a new emphasis on international issues, it shifted to a more right-wing outlook that matched Thomas's own change in political beliefs. However, her vision for *Time and Tide* was not to obtain the maximum number of readers possible, and she was happy to run it at a financial loss. Instead, she was more concerned with the quality of her reader and intended the paper to be a favourite among influential people.

Thomas achieved another milestone in women's history in 1920 when she became one of the first four female Justices of the Peace in the County of Monmouth, though she seldom actually sat. A year later, she launched the Six Point Group (SPG) along with Helen Archdale, which campaigned on six women's rights issues and the rights of children:

- Satisfactory legislation on child assault
- Satisfactory legislation for the widowed mother
- Satisfactory legislation for the unmarried mother and her child
- Equal rights for guardianship for married parents
- Equal pay for teachers
- Equal opportunities for men and women in the Civil Service.

The aim of the Six Point Group later evolved from these specific points to the more general goals of fairness for women, which were political, occupational, moral, social, economic and legal equality. The SPG made a blacklist of politicians who opposed legislation on women's rights. They then urged women to vote against them in the 1922 General Elections, and out of twenty-three MPs running who were on the list, nine were defeated and two stood down. They also lobbied the political parties to end the practice of only putting up female candidates in unwinnable seats. The 16 November 1923 issue of *Time and Tide* noted:

> When the women get defeated … the parties who have thus used them are the first to turn around and say: 'There is no use putting up women candidates, they only get defeated' … It should be remembered that there is no generosity in offering a woman the chance of fighting a hopeless seat on condition that she pays her own expenses.

In 1926, she was the first woman to be appointed president of the Institute of Directors, and in the same year she continued the fight for equal pay and more opportunities in the workplace by founding the Open-Door Council. She also used her influence to organise demonstrations, meetings and discussions with politicians to help create the 1928 Equal Franchise Act that finally achieved the goals that the suffrage organisations had fought for, voting rights on the same terms as men, as well as universal adult suffrage.

After the war, her father was recognised for his service and made Viscount Rhondda, but Margaret inherited the title when he died in July 1918. He also left her a vast amount of money, and she took over as the director of his thirty-three companies, becoming the chairperson of several of them, which gave her the task of overseeing his industrial empire of coalmines, steelworks, shipping companies and newspapers. For a woman to become an heir to all of this is seen as a victory for feminism, as in the first decades of the twentieth century, this type of inheritance was usually reserved for male children.

However, despite now being Viscount Rhondda, she was not allowed to sit, or vote, in the House of Lords by virtue of being a woman. Unsurprisingly, Lady Rhondda did not take this lying down and in 1920, she petitioned to change this under the Sex Disqualification (Removal) Act of 1919, which stated that, 'A woman shall not be disqualified by sex or marriage from the exercise of any public function.' The House of Lords Committee for Privileges favoured the proposal but was overruled by the Lord Chancellor, Lord Birkenhead, in May 1922. George Bernard Shaw was quoted on the subject by Crystal Eastman in the newspaper the *Christian Science Monitor* on 8 March 1922:

> Lady Rhondda is the terror of the House of Lords. She is a peeress in her own right. She is also an extremely capable woman of business, and the House of Lords has risen up and said, 'If Lady Rhondda comes in here, we go

away!' They feel there would be such a show-up of the general business ignorance and imbecility of the male sex as never was before.

She continued to fight, but it was not until 30 April 1958 that women could sit in the House of Lords as life peers. Margaret Haig Thomas died less than three months later on 20 July, before the first women took their seats in the Lords the following October; five years later, hereditary female peers were allowed to sit in the House of Lords with the passing of the Peerage Act of 1963.

Adela – The Pankhurst on the Wrong Side of History

Adela Pankhurst (1885–1961) was the youngest daughter of Emmeline Pankhurst and was involved in the suffrage movement at a very early stage of her middle-class upbringing. She was a sickly child who suffered from lung problems and had to wear splints on her legs, leaving her unable to walk until she was 3 years old. She trained to be a teacher, and by 1903 she was working in an elementary school though her mother was against it as she saw it as a working-class profession. Later that year, Adela would help her mother and sisters, Christabel and Sylvia, form the WSPU. Her contribution is less well known today than her siblings and, in some ways, more problematic, which is why – at least to some extent – she is the forgotten Pankhurst sister.

She quickly gained a reputation as an excellent public speaker and was not afraid to get her hands dirty when it came to militant protests. She was first sent to prison for seven days in June 1906 after being a part of a group of suffragettes who disrupted a Liberal Party meeting. Later the same year, she was part of a group that entered the House of Commons, which led to the arrest of nine women. From 1908, she moved to Scarborough, in the North Riding of Yorkshire, where she protested against visiting politicians, helped open a local branch of the WSPU, and organised and spoke at meetings.

Her beliefs did not always align with those of her mother. She was active in the ILP and would often distribute their literature across Yorkshire, while Emmeline and Christabel had abandoned the idea of an alliance with any political party soon after the conception of their organisation. Adela also believed in universal suffrage and campaigned for equal rights for working-class women, whereas the policy of the WSPU was to enfranchise women on the same terms as men, which would have only included women with substantial financial means or assets at their disposal.

When Winston Churchill was giving a talk in Dundee in October 1909, she was one of three people who hid in the attic and rained bricks and slates down on the venue while others demonstrated outside the hall. When a policeman tried to evict her from the building, she slapped him and was arrested for breaking the peace. She went on a hunger strike but was not force-fed as it was assessed that her heart was too erratic. Like her sister Sylvia, by 1910 Adela believed the militancy of the WSPU was going too far and was hurting the cause. Her health was also in decline at this point having suffered from bronchitis, so in October 1911 she resigned, leading to a falling out with her mother and Christabel.

Over the next few years Adela found work, but her ill health made it difficult to maintain. In February 1914, it was decided that the warmer climate of Australia would benefit her health, so her mother bought her a ticket, gave her £20, and wrote her a letter of recommendation to the suffragist and social reformer Vida Goldstein. Women in her newly adopted country had been able to vote since 1902 with the passage of the Commonwealth Franchise Act, (which excluded Aboriginal and Torres Strait Islander women, who had to wait until 1962 for their right to vote). Despite this and her ill health, Adela Pankhurst was not ready to retire and as soon as she arrived in Australia, she began working with women's rights advocates there.

When war broke out, she was against helping the war effort and joined the Women's Peace Army (WPA) in Melbourne. The group was formed by Vida Goldstein in July 1915 and used the colours of the WSPU, purple, green and white, for their flag. Pankhurst was known as the 'Maid of Peace' in Australia, and wrote anti-war pamphlets and spoke to crowds denouncing the conscription of young Australian men, often being jeered and heckled by soldiers as she did so. She helped establish several branches of the WPA in 1915, and the following year she toured New Zealand and Australia speaking out against the war.

She worked with fellow former suffragette Jennie Baines in 1917 in protesting rising food prices and, while on remand, she married Tom Walsh, a prominent trade unionist and political activist. She was offered the opportunity to walk free by the Australian Prime Minister Billy Hughes on the condition that she never gave another speech, though unsurprisingly she turned the offer down and served a four-month sentence. She worked with Baines again in 1920 to found the Communist Party of Australia, believing it would lead to a new way of living where poverty was a thing of the past, but like Baines, she was later expelled after disagreeing with some of Stalin's policies.

She went on to form the anti-communist organisation, the Australian Women's Guild of Empire (AWGE) in 1928, based on the Women's Guild of Empire in London, which was founded by Flora Drummond in 1920. The AWGE helped raise money for working-class women and children, and Adela and her husband now spoke out against trade unions and industrial action. On several occasions, they crossed picket lines to express their belief that strikes harmed the workers they were supposed to be helping and instead argued in favour of industrial cooperation. She also denounced contraception, abortion and was against the use of nursery schools as she believed they undermined maternal instincts and parental responsibilities.

In December 1939, the pair visited Japan, reflecting their belief that Australia should be allied with them as trade partners over America. By 1941 her politics had shifted entirely, and she helped form the far-right nationalistic, Australia First Movement (AFM) that supported fascism and Nazism. The organisation was anti-British, may have been antisemitic, and favoured joining the Axis powers at the start of the

Second World War. Pankhurst was arrested along with many members of the AFM after the attack on Pearl Harbor in 1941 and she reverted to the old tactic of going on hunger strike, which led to her being released after two days. The following year she was taken to a camp for political prisoners where she was held for several months. The AFM was dissolved soon after in 1942 and after the death of her husband in April 1943, she ceased her political activities and retired from public life.

It is easy to judge the choices of Adela Pankhurst with hindsight and realise that when compared to the likes of Margaret Haig Thomas, she was on the wrong side of history. It should, however, be remembered that throughout her activist career, she remained committed to fighting for equality for men and women, especially for those from the working-classes. Her life story serves as a poignant reminder that the path to social progress is often unclear until we look back, and that open dialogue and consideration of diverse ideas are key. It should also be remembered that people, past and present, should be judged on their merit and their overall motivations, not just on their failures and mistakes. Before she died in 1928, Emmeline Pankhurst reached out and expressed to her daughter that she regretted the long-running conflict between them. She would never see her daughter again and never met her eight grandchildren. Adela died in May 1961 aged 75, a year after converting to Catholicism.

The Legacy of the Suffrage Movement

By the time the Representation of the People Act (1918) was enacted, suffrage societies had been fighting for over fifty years. After so many broken promises, imprisonment and even deaths, they finally achieved political power through the vote and the right to become Members of Parliament through the Parliament (Qualification of Women) Act (1918). After the Equal Franchise Act (1928), 15 million women were eligible to vote, and for the first time, women became the majority of voters in Britain, making up a little under 53 per cent of the electorate.

How much the militant actions of the suffragettes helped to win the vote is hotly debated. Some believe that it set the cause back as many politicians stopped engaging with suffrage campaigners. It certainly turned off many members of the public, with some disapproving of the methods on moral grounds and others believing that by committing militant and violent acts, they were demonstrating the type of emotional outbursts that it was thought would make them ineffectual voters. However, peaceful methods had been failing for over forty years before the militant campaign started, and it is undeniable that the suffragettes brought the issue of female suffrage to the forefront of people's minds with the amount of publicity they won. This, coupled with the work done by the various suffrage societies and the contribution of women generally during the First World War, helped the idea of women's suffrage on the same terms as men take hold and to be eventually won.

Part of the suffragettes' legacy is that for the first time a generation of girls grew up seeing women in the media as strong, independent leaders who were willing to fight for what they believed in. While women like this have always existed, the propaganda techniques used by suffrage societies, particularly the WSPU, made it possible for more young girls of that nature to have role models, paving the way for future activists. The vote in and of itself was what was deemed necessary to achieve the other goals of the broader women's movement. Reproductive rights, equal pay and fair treatment in the workplace were all issues that it was believed the vote would help with, and while these topics are still debated today it cannot be denied that significant progress has been made in the hundred years or so since the vote was won, compared with the centuries that preceded the suffrage movement.

Although women's suffrage was a fiercely debated subject by anti-suffrage campaigners and between suffrage groups, everyone knew that if it came into being, a lot would change. Its most optimistic supporters believed it could end war and poverty, and Christabel Pankhurst wrote in her book *The Great Scourge and*

How to End It (1913), that women's suffrage could even help end STDs. Alternatively, those who were most ardently against women's suffrage believed it would mean the end of family values and the destruction of morals within society. Some argued that in reality, very little changed after the vote was won. Virginia Woolf believed that money was the most critical asset for a woman. In an essay entitled *Room of One's Own* (1929), she stated:

> Intellectual freedom depends upon material things … And women have always been poor, not for two hundred years merely, but from the beginning of time … The news of my legacy reached me one night about the same time the act passed that gave votes to women … Of the two, the vote and the money, the money, I own, seemed infinitely the more important.

After the First World War, most women left the jobs that were traditionally men's work and returned to their old lives. During the Second World War, the women of Britain were again instrumental in the war effort by picking up the jobs of the men who were off fighting, and helped make the munitions they needed to fight. Women could also join the armed forces, and when the war was over many stayed in employment – though they would earn less than their male counterparts for another thirty years. Change came when a group of women who worked at the Ford sewing machine factory in Dagenham went on strike in 1968. They demanded equal pay as they were paid around 15 per cent less than men doing the same work, which was common practice at the time. The strikers won, and in the following year the victory inspired female trade unionists to hold an equal pay demonstration in Trafalgar Square, both of which helped pave the way for the passing of the Equal Pay Act of 1970 (enacted in 1975). While it is true that a gender pay gap still exists today, when factors such as the number of hours worked, unsociable hours, the undesirability of a job and dangerous conditions are taken into consideration, the gap all but disappears and it is illegal to pay anybody less money based solely on their gender.

The activists of the early women's movement, often now called first-wave feminists, focused on absolute rights such as winning the vote. This allowed feminists from the 1960s to the end of the 1980s, otherwise known as second wave feminists or members of the women's liberation movement, to focus on more nuanced aspects of women's rights such as fair pay and opportunities in the workplace, equal rights in law and autonomy over their own bodies through abortion rights and birth control.

Women gained a lot more control over their lives from the early 1960s with the development of the contraceptive pill, which was made available on the NHS in December 1961, along with advances in latex condoms and the introduction of plastic intrauterine devices. They allowed for greater sexual freedom for both men and women, and helped advance the women's liberation movement. In the same decade in 1967, abortion was legalised in Britain, before which backstreet abortions were one of the leading causes of maternal deaths. In 1975, the Sex Discrimination Act helped prevent discrimination and harassment based on gender in the workplace, in education and with the supply of goods and services, all of which were issues that suffrage activists in the early twentieth century believed the vote for women would help end.

Third-wave feminism took the nuances further and added intersectionality to the issues, conflating gender with other social categorisations such as class, race and sexual orientation. Although these issues manifested during the struggle for the vote, it was only by the late 1980s to the early 1990s that they started to come to the forefront of the women's movement. Modern feminism, or fourth-wave feminism, began around 2008 and seeks to use modern technology such as the internet to deliver its message. It adds far-left politics, psychology and spirituality to intersectionality and tends to focus on some older issues, such as reproductive rights and the improvement of children's services, as well as newer issues such as body positivity, the acceptance, and the well-being, of sex workers, and transgender rights.

As always, there is division in the women's movement from within. Transgender issues are at the forefront of this in the 2020s, with some feminists being critical of their participation in women's sports and their use of women's toilets and changing rooms. Fourth-wave feminists call these people 'Trans Exclusionary Radical Feminists' (TERFs), though this is often seen as derogatory, and the term 'gender critical' is preferred. In turn, fourth-wave feminists are frequently called 'woke' in a pejorative way, especially by people on the political centre or the right, even though the term has a long history of being used positively to describe various types of progressive thought.

The tactics of the WSPU continue to inspire feminism and the fight for equal rights to this day, as well as other types of activism. On the issue of climate change and the environment, there are protesters such as Greta Thunberg, a teenager who is willing to stand in front of politicians and industry leaders and call them out in speeches and demonstrations, and willing to get arrested for civil disobedience, much like the early suffragettes did. On the other hand, there are the Just Stop Oil protesters who replicate some of the more militant (though non-violent) tactics of the WSPU, such as civil resistance, obstructing traffic and vandalism, with many members of the group being sent to prison. When two protestors threw tomato soup on Vincent van Gogh's 1888 work *The Arles Sunflowers* in the National Gallery, the two were sent to prison for damage caused to the frame (as the painting itself was encased in glass). The act caused public outcry and was condemned, but it did garner a great deal of media coverage for Just Stop Oil and has been compared the actions of Mary Richardson when she slashed the Rokeby Venus in March 1914.

The progress that has been made in the last 160 years or so since the Kensington Society was formed in 1865 by the likes of Barbara Bodichon and Lydia Becker, cannot be overstated. Today, more women sit in the Houses of Commons than ever before, and after the

2024 General Election, 263 of the 650 seats in the House of Commons, or 40 per cent, are held by female MPs. The struggle for equality continues and as it was with the suffragists and the suffragettes, feminists still often disagree on what the path to progress should entail. Despite this, the foundation of the cause is still the same, equal rights for, and the fair treatment of, women within British society and beyond.

The ultimate appeal on a disputed question of policy is not now made to the swords of the people, but to their votes. Rival politicians do not ask one another how many men each can send into the field, but how many votes each can count at the polling-booth. Should there arise a dispute as to the succession to the throne, the War of the Roses of the present period would be fought, not on the battlefield, but at the ballot-box. It is this mighty change which has rendered possible the political equality of women with men and made it practicable to secure for them the protection which is necessary for their security, development and the future progress of the race. For a vote, unlike a sword, is a weapon which is as potent in the hands of a woman as in that of a man.

Lydia Becker. *Words of a Leader*.
The Central Society for
Women's Suffrage (1904).

Conclusion

Although the idea of female enfranchisement has been around for hundreds of years, it was not until the 1830s that it began to be discussed in the British political arena. Over the next forty years or so pioneers such as Barbara Bodichon and Lydia Becker campaigned on feminist issues, including a married woman's right to own property, a woman's right to earn her own money, and the right to a decent education for girls, especially for those from poorer backgrounds. Activists soon came to realise that the only way to achieve these objectives was for women to gain the vote and in 1867, the National Society for Women's Suffrage became a precursor to the numerous suffrage organisations that would emerge in the following decades. The individuals involved would lobby politicians, hold meetings, write and distribute various types of literature and draw up petitions to advance the cause, actions that would have been considered radical by many people when executed by women.

While there was a degree of unity among members of the suffrage societies, the groups themselves began to fracture over disagreements on key issues, such as who should lead them, which political party to align with (if any), and which women should initially be enfranchised. With the formation of the National Union of Women's Suffrage Societies (NUWSS) in 1897, the movement became more coherent. Millicent Garrett Fawcett led the group along the same lines as earlier suffrage groups, employing peaceful means of protest, which she referred to as constitutional lobbying. Unhappy with the progress being made by the NUWSS, Emmeline Pankhurst and her daughters formed the breakaway group, the Women's Social and Political Union (WSPU) in 1903. They believed that constitutional lobbying had proved ineffective, and it was time for a more militant strategy, or what Fawcett called 'revolutionary lobbying'. This included marching on the Houses of Parliament, interrupting meetings and accosting MPs, and later would consist of damaging property, arson and bombing buildings.

Other suffrage groups would also form, often based on occupation, such as the Artists' Suffrage League (ASL), the Actress's Franchise League (AFL) and the Women Writers' Suffrage League (WWSL). Others still formed as breakaway groups, such as the Women's Freedom League (WFL), which split from the WSPU in 1907. However, to some extent most groups were usually allied with the NUWSS, the WSPU, or both. As most people in the country opposed women's suffrage in the late nineteenth and early twentieth century, anti-suffrage groups inevitably formed. They were comprised of both men and women from all walks of life and objected on various grounds. Some believed that female enfranchisement would win extra votes for political parties other than the ones to which they were affiliated. Others thought it would lead to neglect of the home and family, while others still doubted the intellectual capacity and political knowledge of British women.

Both supporters and opponents of female suffrage launched a propaganda campaign aimed at influencing popular opinion among the general public. Everything from postcards, posters, plays and articles were used to send out the messages of the various groups. The activism of the WSPU intensified in 1905 when Annie Kenney and Christabel Pankhurst became the first suffragettes to be arrested for the cause. The incident, arrest and subsequent prison sentences became worldwide news, bringing the idea of female suffrage to many who had not previously considered it and gaining many supporters – not only for the WSPU, but also for the movement in general. Militant action became the most effective strategy for the WSPU's propaganda campaign from this point forward, as it consistently gained them coverage in national and even international newspapers.

Not content to trust other newspapers to report on their actions accurately, suffrage groups also published their own journals, such as *The Common Cause*, produced by the NUWSS and *Votes for Women*, and later *The Suffragette*, both of which belonged to the WSPU. Another way to boost the propaganda campaign was by finding unusual, headline-grabbing ways to protest against MPs. This was usually done by the more interesting and often flamboyant members of the WSPU such as Annie Kenney, who would wear the traditional clothes of a mill worker to demonstrations, and Flora Drummond, who led processions dressed in military-style attire and riding on a large horse.

Initially, the suffrage movement was predominantly composed of middle-class women, but this would change in the early years of the twentieth century. Annie Kenney became a leading figure in the movement, focusing on gaining support from working-class women. As time went on, more attention was given to attracting new members from the middle and upper classes, as they would generally have more money to help support the organisations and be less likely to need to work, allowing them to devote more time to the cause. When exceptionally affluent women such as Lady Constance Lytton and Princess Sophia Duleep Singh were involved in protests, it was considered extremely newsworthy by the press and, as an added bonus, served as an embarrassment to the government and their elitist peers.

The movement transcended the norms of social class, and close friendships were formed across the class divide as women bonded through campaigning and serving prison time together, sometimes forming lifelong friendships in the process. Although class distinction was less important to those within the cause than it would generally be, this was not true of the authorities. Princess Sophia Duleep Singh could not get herself arrested – though not for the want of trying – and when Lady Constance Lytton was first arrested, she noticed she was treated differently from working-class and middle-class inmates. When she tested this theory by disguising herself as the working-class seamstress Jane Warton, she was treated much more harshly, as she had suspected she would be, even enduring bouts of force-feeding, something she had previously been spared.

Starting with Marion Wallace-Dunlop, suffragettes began going on hunger strike when in prison to protest the lack of political status awarded to them. Initially, this would result in early release once they fell ill due to the lack of nourishment, but in the summer of 1909, Evaline Hilda Burkitt became the first suffragette to be force-fed in prison. Although the practice was seen as unethical even by many people opposed to the WSPU or their militant actions, forcing food through nasal or stomach tubes became standard practice, though the suffragettes were undeterred by this and continued to refuse food. To combat this, the government introduced the Cat and Mouse Act, allowing women to be released to recover before being rearrested. The suffragettes managed to make the most of this legislation and added thirst and sleep strikes to facilitate an even earlier release. Many would then be able to avoid rearrest altogether, and others would be sure to commit another act of militant protest before they could be taken back to prison.

Hope of at least a partial victory came in early 1910 in the form of the proposed Conciliation Bill, which would have given around 1.5 million women the opportunity to vote in general elections. To help the bill pass, the WSPU called a truce and ceased all militant action for the foreseeable future, although they continued to participate in peaceful protests. The Black Friday protest in November 1910 turned into chaos, with suffragettes attacking, and being assaulted by, the police, but after a few days the truce was restored to give the Conciliation Bill a good chance of success. This did not last long, however, and when the WSPU leadership lost faith in the bill as a viable option in late 1911, they resumed their militant campaign.

Over the next two-and-a-half years, vandalism and violent protests would escalate. It began with coordinated attacks smashing multiple windows in London and soon intensified to a campaign that included arson and bombings. Some describe this extreme militancy as terrorism, while others see it as a legitimate form of protest conducted by freedom fighters. The press and the public of the time were not impressed and many who had supported, or at least sympathised with, the organisation now turned on them and, by extension, the movement in general. This was offset to some extent by the NUWSS, which continued to lobby MPs peacefully and made some headway in these years, though, as always, it was the militant actions of the WSPU that continued to make most of the headlines.

When the First World War broke out, the WSPU suspended its activism and put its considerable organisational and fundraising skills to good use in supporting the war effort. The leaders focused on getting women into the workplace, while many individual members from the rank and file helped in any way they could. Some became nurses or administrators, and even entertained the troops, while others worked in factories in place of the men fighting the war, or helped to make munitions.

The Representation of the People Act of 1918 enabled some women over the age of 30 to vote. While this led to many suffrage organisations disbanding and many activists leaving the movement altogether, many more fought on to achieve the goal of gaining votes on the same terms as men. This was finally accomplished, along with universal adult suffrage, with the Equal Franchise Act of 1928, again prompting many to leave the struggle believing the fight was finally won. Other suffrage campaigners, such as Margaret Haig Thomas, however, realised that this was just the beginning and that the fight for equal rights in law, the workplace, in education and within British society in general had only just begun.

While it is true to say that the struggle continues to this day, great strides have been made since the first suffrage societies formed to fight for women's rights. Much of the acclaim for this progress rightly goes to the leaders of the late nineteenth and early twentieth-century movement, in particular Emmeline Pankhurst and Millicent

Garrett Fawcett. However, a great deal of credit should also go to the thousands of other women who contributed to the cause in large and small ways, who sacrificed their time, money, freedom and sometimes even their lives. The forgotten heroes of the British suffrage movement, both militant and constitutional alike, who changed the world by winning their objective, 'to obtain the parliamentary franchise on the same terms as it is, or may be, granted to men'. so that the broader objectives of the women's movement could be fought for and achieved, providing us with a fairer, more egalitarian society today.

Bibliography

Secondary Sources

Atkinson, D., 2018. *Rise Up Women – The Remarkable Lives of the Suffragettes*. Bloomsbury. London.

Bartley, P., 1998. *Votes for Women 1860–1928*. Hodder & Stoughton. London.

Crawford, E., 2000. *The Women's Suffrage Movement – A Reference Guide*. Routledge. London.

Hawksley, L., 2013. *March, Women, March – Voices of the Women's Movement from the First Feminist to Votes for Women*. Andre Deutsch Limited. London.

Holten, S., 1996. *Suffrage Days – Stories from the Women's Suffrage Movement*. Routledge. London.

Kent, S.K., 1990. *Sex and Suffrage in Britain, 1860–1914*. Routledge. London.

Liddington, J. & Norris, J., 2000. *One Hand Tied Behind Us – The Rise of the Women's Suffrage Movement*. Rivers Oram Press. Barcombe.

Marlow, J., 2000. *Suffragettes – The Fight for Votes for Women*. Virago Press. London.

Pugh, M., 2002. *The March of the Women: A Revisionist Analysis of the Campaign for Women's Suffrage, 1866–1914*. Oxford University Press. Oxford.

Riddle, F., 2018. *Death in Ten Minutes – Kitty Marion Activist. Arsonist. Suffragette*. Hodder & Stoughton. London.

Robinson, J., 2018. *Hearts and Minds – The Untold Story of the Great Pilgrimage and How Women Won the Vote.* Penguin. London.

Primary Sources

Becker, L. [Internet]. 1904. (Second Edition). *Words of a Leader – Being Extracts from the Writings of the late Miss Lydia Becker.* The Central Society for Women's Suffrage. London. Available From: https://mlfhs.uk/oldham/research/speakers-notes/1980-lydia-becker-words-of-a-leader/file [Accessed 15/05/2025].

Billington-Greig, T. [Internet]. 1911. *The Militant Suffrage Movement – Emancipation in a Hurry.* F Palmer. London. Available From: https://archive.org/details/militantsuffrage00tere [Accessed 15/05/2025].

Bodichon, B. [Internet]. 1866. *Reasons for the Enfranchisement of Women.* National Association for the Promotion of Social Science. London. Available From: https://archive.org/details/reasonsforenfran00bodi [Accessed 15/05/2025].

Codd, C. [Internet]. 1951. *So Rich a Life.* Caxton Limited. South Africa. Available From: https://archive.org/details/CoddSoRichALife/page/n5/mode/2up [Accessed 15/05/2025].

Garrud, E. [Internet]. 1910. 'Damsel v. Desperado'. *Health & Strength Magazine.* United Kingdom. Available From: https://ejmas.com/jnc/jncart_garrud_1299.htm [Accessed 15/05/2025].

Kenney, A. [Internet]. 1924. *Memories of a Militant.* Edward Arnold and Co. London. Available From: https://archive.org/details/in.ernet.dli.2015.201549 [Accessed 15/05/2025].

Lowndes, M. [Internet]. 1909. *Banners and Banner Making.* The Artist's Suffrage League. Chelsea. Available From: www.flickr.com/photos/lselibrary/24723714138/in/photostream [Accessed 15/05/2025].

Lytton, C. [Internet]. 1914. *Prisons and Prisoners: Some Personal Experiences.* William Heinemann. London.

Available From: https://digital.library.upenn.edu/women/lytton/prisons/prisons.html [Accessed 15/05/2025].

McLaren, L. [Internet]. 1909. *The Women's charter of rights & liberties – Preliminary Draft*. J. Sewell. London. Available From: https://archive.org/details/womenscharterofr00aberuoft/mode/2up [Accessed 15/05/2025].

Montefiore, D. [Internet]. 1896. *Why We Need Woman's Suffrage, and Why We Need It Now*. Shafts. United Kingdom. Available From: www.marxists.org/archive/montefiore/1896/woman-suffrage.htm [Accessed 15/05/2025].

Montefiore, D. [Internet]. 1925. *From a Victorian to a Modern*. E. Archer. London. Available From: www.marxists.org/archive/montefiore/1925/autobiography/index.htm [Accessed 15/05/2025].

Pankhurst, E. [Internet]. 1914. *My Own Story*. London Eveleigh Nash. London. Available From: www.gutenberg.org/files/34856/34856-h/34856-h.htm [Accessed 15/05/2025].

Pankhurst, S. [Internet]. 1931. *The Suffragette Movement – An Intimate Account of Persons and Ideals*. Longmans, Green and Co. London. Available From: https://archive.org/details/suffragettemovem0000pank_k6o1/mode/2up [Accessed 15/05/2025].

Wollstonecraft, M. [Internet]. 1792. *A Vindication of the Rights of Women – With Strictures on Political and Moral Subjects*. J. Johnson. London. Available From: www.google.co.uk/books/edition/A_Vindication_of_the_Rights_of_Woman/hxwEAAAAYAAJ?hl=en&gbpv=1 [Accessed 15/05/2025].

Online Resources

Exploring Surrey's Past. (www.exploringsurreyspast.org.uk).
How the Vote was Won. (www.thesuffragettes.org).
London Museum. (www.londonmuseum.org.uk).
LSE History. (https://blogs.lse.ac.uk).

Spartacus Educational. (https://spartacus-educational.com).

Suffragette Stories. (https://suffragettestories.omeka.net).

The History of Fighting. (www.historyoffighting.com).

The National Archives. (www.nationalarchives.gov.uk).

The National Trust. (www.nationaltrust.org.uk).

The UK Parliament. (www.parliament.uk).

Time and Tide. (https://timeandtidemagazine.org).

Towards Emancipation. (https://hist259.web.unc.edu).

Woman and Her Sphere. (https://womanandhersphere.com).

Women's Suffrage. (www.suffrageresources.org.uk).

Selected Online Articles

Atkinson, D. [Internet]. 2017. 'Six Inspiring Suffragettes You Probably Haven't Heard Of'. *Stylist*. Available From: https://www.stylist.co.uk/visible-women/suffragettes-less-famous-sophia-singh-mary-gawthorpe-rachel-barrett-annie-kenney-kitty-marion-lavender-guthrie/188021 [Accessed 15/05/2025].

Baker, L. [Internet]. 2024. *In History: Suffragettes Speak About Direct Action and Their Brutal Treatment.* BBC Culture. Available From: www.bbc.co.uk/culture/article/20240307-in-history-suffragettes-speak-about-direct-action-and-their-brutal-treatment [Accessed 15/05/2025].

Graham, S. [Internet]. 2025. *Helen Pankhurst on How the Suffragettes' Actions Still Inspire Today.* Google Arts and Culture. Available From: https://artsandculture.google.com/story/helen-pankhurst-on-how-the-suffragettes-actions-still-inspire-today/dAURzTsRJLg6Ig?hl=en [Accessed 15/05/2025].

Jenkins, L. [Internet]. 2019. *Annie Kenney and the Politics of Class in the Women's Social and Political Union.* Oxford Academy. Available From: https://academic.oup.com/tcbh/article/30/4/477/5569516 [Accessed 15/05/2025].

Lewsey, F. [Internet]. 2025. *Our Weapon is Public Opinion – Posters of the Women's Suffrage Movement at the University*

Library. The University of Cambridge. Available From: www.cam.ac.uk/stories/suffrage [Accessed 15/05/2025].

Mohan, M. [Internet]. 2018. *Kitty Marion: The Actress Who Became a 'Terrorist.'* BBC News. Available From: www.bbc.co.uk/news/stories-44210012 [Accessed 15/05/2025].

Shedden, K. [Internet]. 2023. *Flora McKinnon Drummond – the General and the Suffragettes.* London Guided Walks. Available From: https://londonguidedwalks.co.uk/flora-mckinnon-drummond-the-general-and-the-suffragettes [Accessed 15/05/2025].

The Formation of the National Society for Women's Suffrage (NSWS). [Internet]. 2025. Cove. Available From: https://editions.covecollective.org/chronologies/formation-national-society-women%E2%80%99s-suffrage-nsws [Accessed 15/05/2025].

The Great Miss Lydia Becker: Suffragist, Scientist and Trailblazer. [Internet]. 2022. Chetham's Library. Available From: https://library.chethams.com/blog/the-great-miss-lydia-becker-suffragist-scientist-and-trailblazer [Accessed 15/05/2025].